C20

Bristol's Twentieth-Century Buildings

This book is dedicated to Peter Ware RIBA, 1929-1999.

Peter Ware was always passionate about Bristol - the city where he lived all his life and where he set up practice in the early 1960s. He was rare amongst architects in combining an enthusiasm for the new with a deep love and knowledge of the old. His most significant work may well prove to have been his great restoration works at Acton Court, at Barleston Hall, or at Clevedon Pier, but there was also his much admired and enjoyed contemporary work such as that at Bristol Zoo.

Peter's very close relationships with both his clients and his builders made him a natural enthusiast for the Architecture Centre, dedicated as it is to the promotion and wider awareness of the art and craft of his discipline.

As a very active Trustee and latterly vice Chairman of the Centre, Peter was closely involved in its initiation and development. Following his untimely death, the Trustees were very pleased that his family asked that money provided in his memory should be given to the Centre. Peter was well aware of plans for this book and we know that he would have approved of this fund being put towards the production of a project that both celebrates the architecture of his city and also promotes the aims and objectives of the Architecture Centre itself.

David Mellor, Chairman of Trustees April 2000

C20

Bristol's Twentieth-Century Buildings

Tony Aldous, with photographs
by John Trelawny-Ross

The Architecture Centre

In association with Redcliffe Press

First published in 2000 for Bristol Centre for the Advancement of Architecture by
Redcliffe Press Ltd., 81g Pembroke Road, Bristol BS8 3EA

© text — Tony Aldous
© photographs — John Trelawny-Ross

ISBN 1 900178 62 1
British Library Cataloguing in Publication Data:
A catalogue record for this book is available from The British Library

Designed by Gendall Design, Falmouth, Cornwall and printed by WBC Ltd., Bridgend,
Mid Glamorgan

Contents

Credits *2*

Foreword *3*

Introduction *4*

1 The First Two Decades: 1900-1919 *10*

2 The Inter-War Years: 1920-1939 *26*

3 Brave New World: 1940-1959 *38*

4 Swinging Sixties: 1960-1969 *44*

5 The Rise of Conservation: 1970-1979 *52*

6 Urban Repair and Conservation: 1980-1989 *68*

7 Changing Gear: 1990-1999 *82*

8 Millennium Landmarks *122*

Envoi: into the 21st Century *132*

Acknowledgements *133*

Index of buildings and places *134*

Index of architects, designers, landscape architects and artists *136*

Maps *138-139*

Credits

The production of this book has only
been possible thanks to generous
financial support for which the Trustees
are extremely grateful.

The major sponsors are:
Bristol City Council
The University of Bristol
The Peter Ware Memorial Fund

Subscriptions have been received from the
following:
Alan Baxter and Associates
Alec French Partnership
Architecton
Badminton School
Banks Wood & Partners
BGP McConaghy Architects
Bovis Ltd
Bristol Water PLC
Bruges Tozer Partnership

Chris Wilkinson Architects
Davis Langdon & Everest
Feilden Clegg Design
Ferguson Mann Architects
Inscape Architects
Kenneth Brown & Partners
Lloyds TSB
MacCormac Jamieson Prichard
Marriott Hotels
Michael Hopkins & Partners
Nicholas Grimshaw & Partners
Percy Thomas Partnership
RAC Motoring Services
River Station Restaurant
Sir Robert McAlpine Ltd
Stride Treglown
Structures 1
Symonds Group
Vic Love Architects
Wessex Water PLC

Foreword

Part of Bristol's fascination is undoubtedly its architecture. I know of no other provincial city which can compare in terms of the sheer variety of architectural styles and the number of distinguished (or attractively quirky) buildings. Consider that architecture in tandem with the city's unique topography and you begin to understand the secret of Bristol's powerful appeal.

Now that we have entered the twenty-first century, it is fitting to look back at the legacy of the previous one. Although Bristol dates back a thousand years, many of its architectural treasures are of relatively recent vintage. They deserve to be celebrated, and this book does so in a way which will delight all those who love Bristol and relish its extraordinary character.

Councillor Graham Robertson
The Rt Hon The Lord Mayor of Bristol

The twentieth century saw many splendid, and not a few disastrous, buildings in Bristol, and it is good to have this excellent compendium to celebrate the variety and energy of the townscape. The University, which is such a prominent feature of the City of Bristol, and which benefits so much from being at its heart, is glad to be associated with this timely book. We may not agree with all the opinions, but we accept the challenge to build in a way that adds to, rather than damages, the rich environment of Bristol. May the twenty-first century do even better.

Sir John Kingman FRS
Vice Chancellor, University of Bristol

Introduction

This book comes about for two reasons. The first goes back to the late 1970s, when John Sansom of Redcliffe Press approached me on behalf of Bristol Civic Society to write a book for them about recent new buildings and conservation schemes in the Bristol area. Published in 1980 as *Changing Bristol: New Architecture and Conservation 1960-1980*, that book, despite its shortcomings, received an enthusiastic welcome. It must have proved useful to some people, for from about 1990 onwards I could scarcely put a foot in Bristol without someone saying, "You know, that book's getting very out of date. Can't you write another one?"

The answer was, of course, that books cost money to publish, and authors are generally not these days prepared to starve in garrets - even the garrets of Georgian terraces! If Bristolians wanted an update, might they not perhaps produce the funding to make it possible? No-one did. And then Bristol got itself an Architecture Centre, and the Architecture Centre got itself Sasha Lubetkin, and Sasha (whom I had known for many years and always found stimulating company) said, "Why not! Let's work on it".

She got hold of the money, not for a book, but for an exhibition. This was to consist of around 100 photographs by John Trelawny-Ross, with accompanying text by me. The theme was Bristol's 20th century buildings, and the funding came from the Arts Council. We soon, however, discovered that 100 buildings were too many: the money wouldn't stretch that far, and the

Architecture Centre's first floor gallery couldn't comfortably hold them. So we settled for an exhibition of 40 panels covering about 60 buildings.

That exhibition, beautifully made a reality by designer Jon Ogborne of Eatcake, is the second reason for this book. It has been remarkably popular, going into second and third showings. There are, I think, at least three reasons for this. First, it was about Bristol, so - either from love or masochism - Bristolians were drawn to it. Secondly, John Trelawny-Ross's photographs, specially taken for it, are a delight; though he did not always enthuse about my choice of buildings, he brought an architect's as well as a photographer's eye to capturing each building's qualities and distinctive personality.

And the third reason? This, it has been suggested to me, has something to do with my own, essentially layman's approach to writing about buildings. As in writing (or talking) about any specialist subject, there is an ever-present danger of overloading your text with technical terms, so that the general reader loses confidence in his ability to follow what you say. The habit of striving not to do that may have helped to make my text for the C20 exhibition relatively concise and approachable.

Lay interpreters of architecture are certainly needed. All too many architects - like practitioners in other specialist fields - find it difficult to describe what they are doing in non-specialist terms. It is true that non-specialist language often lacks the precision needed in the practice of architecture. But that does not mean you need to use a string of technical terms to describe and comment on the results of that practice. Indeed, if you do, you risk losing your lay audience - and if you wish to influence the quality of the built environment, then you cannot afford to lose that audience, for it includes developers, funders of development, members of planning committees, and the much wider lay public whose approval or disapproval can make or mar a scheme's realisation.

It is no longer sufficient for architects to believe in quality and produce quality proposals; they now need to convince an interested and increasingly vocal lay public of that quality. Some of the best architects are brilliant exponents of their work and can explain what they do without jargon's fatal encumbrance. Others lack this ability. Their fingers may be eloquent on drawing board or in computer-aided design, but in talking or writing about their projects they stumble and lose their audience before they even begin to make key points.

By contrast, the journalist's knack and skill is to cut through jargon and get quickly to the point, even at the risk of appearing facile or asking what appear to be stupid questions. There is still a great need to make architecture more approachable, more intelligible to the general public; to show that it is relevant and important to lay people, and that they need not be afraid of discussing it and arguing about it. But at the same time, the writer who tackles this most necessary task of interpreter also has a duty not to gloss over the complications and difficulties of architectural practice, nor to be too populist. Clarity of interpretation does not justify over-simplification, nor swimming with the tide of prejudice. If a good scheme is threatened by opponents who have not understood it, the challenge is not just to champion that scheme but to try to open eyes and change minds which may appear already closed to rational argument.

The exhibition was a success, but what of the book? With Sasha departed, it was the Architecture Centre's chairman David Mellor who threw himself into the task of raising sponsorship. We wanted a book both because it would provide a permanent, more easily accessible record, and because it would allow us to bring back those 40 buildings we had reluctantly excluded from the exhibition. We could even add a few more. A book also provided an opportunity, in this Introduction, for a wider look at architecture and planning in Bristol, and an opportunity to look a little at the role of the client in architecture. This role can be crucial.

In the first three decades of the century, for instance, the preferences of one rich and powerful client, the Wills family, gave Bristol a string of neo-gothic University buildings - stylistically backward-looking but nonetheless splendid and serviceable; while in the same period an enlightened private client commissioned Connell & Ward to design what must have been the quite shockingly modern Concrete House at Westbury.

More recently the 1980s and '90s provide examples of enlightened and unenlightened clients. One example of a good client is the Bristol Royal Society for the Blind. The BRSB provided its architects with an extended course of education into the needs of visually-impaired people which bore fruit in its admirable Bedminster building. By contrast, the original developer of Aztec West, the pension fund ESN, appears to have asked one nationally known architect simply to repeat a design he had done in the very different circumstances of north-west London. The design of a building ought, of course, to spring from the character of the site and the functions and activities it will house.

With the benefit of hindsight, the story of Bristol's 20th century buildings might almost be characterised as a series of hard-won steps forward into modernism or functionalism, matched by sudden lurches back towards the more ornate, highly decorated modes of the 19th century. Except that nothing is nearly as simple as that. Some of the stylistically backward-looking buildings (Oatley at his best, for instance) are widely and justly admired and have proved surprisingly functional, even with changed uses. By contrast, some of the supposedly functional office buildings of the '70s and '80s have worn very badly and are popular neither with their users nor the public.

So how do we define a successful building? What makes for its acceptance by an increasingly interested but critical public, and by increasingly demanding users? For the users, efficiency in operation is clearly a key factor, but so is ambience. Is the building welcoming, does it have "good vibes"? The Bedminster Vision Care Centre clearly does; so in a different way does the radical refurbishment of rented housing at Orlebar Gardens - where before upgrading the vibes were anything but good.

And part of the art of making good vibes has to do with the harmonious or stimulating arrangement of spaces, internal and external. One of the most frustrating experiences of those who, all over the country, serve on planning committees or conservation advisory panels is to see, again and again, plans submitted with elevations of buildings shown in isolation. It is as if they had no context. Yet there are neighbouring buildings and neighbouring spaces, and good new buildings need to be good neighbours.

That is not to say they should be slavishly conformist. In some contexts, to match is the right answer; in many others, contrast - great or small, but well-considered - is the best mark of respect. And as for open spaces, as far as possible buildings should relate to and enhance them: the public space is in a sense more important than the buildings round it. Buildings should complement well designed public spaces; all too often they grudgingly concede awkward scraps of left-over space to the public realm.

So how has Bristol performed when measured against criteria such as these? At times, appallingly. Parts of the city centre - notably around Lewins Mead and Rupert Street - still show the fruits of an approach based on three inter-acting misconceptions: that brutalism in materials and townscape could produce an acceptable urban environment; that exiling pedestrians to upper level walkways could solve traffic problems or be acceptable to people on foot; and that large-scale, clean-sweep redevelopment without regard for existing architectural context could create a splendid new central area. The earlier post-war development of a new shopping centre at Broadmead has been rightly criticised for its subtopian architectural character and initial failure to separate vehicles and pedestrians, but at least it was human-scale.

Trouble with roads was not new to Bristol. The blindness of successive city engineers to the considerations of urban design showed itself most blatantly in the 1930s when one of them thrust a dual carriageway diagonally through Bristol's grandest public space, Queen Square - a brutal assault which, happily, is now being remedied. Even greater blindness to public amenity showed itself in a 1970s city council's determination to fill in most of the Floating Harbour so as to create land for new office blocks and road systems. In mitigation it should be added that all over the country at that time, developers and planning authorities were ignoring the recreational and development potential of waterside settings and treating canals, quaysides and dock basins as their scrapyards and dustbins. In very many cases, it was largely the difficulty and expense of providing substitute land drainage systems that saved waterways from extinction or burial in culverts.

In Bristol this short-sighted strategy was thwarted - as were several others - by the determined efforts of a group of public-spirited and environmentally enlightened citizens. A small minority cared enough to say, "This is not cut and dried. We can and must prevent it". And - thanks to their formidable collective expertise in planning, urban design, law and other specialisms -

they succeeded. Now that the watersides of the Floating Harbour have been opened up with restaurants, bars, shops, and heritage and tourist attractions, with the familiar yellow-and-blue ferries busily plying to and fro, we can see what a huge debt Bristol owes to those citizens who refused to accept the seemingly inevitable.

Which brings me to the Bristol Civic Society. Over the years, day in, day out, the society has made a cumulative contribution of immense importance to the appearance and amenity of the city - not just by opposing the bad and misguided, but by innovative thinking and promotion of positive improvements. It has questioned, argued, persuaded, lobbied; opened the public's eyes to what is and what might be; and striven to achieve the difficult balance of supporting adventurous design while retaining the support of an often over-cautious and conservative public opinion. The big break-through in public perception has arguably been the acceptance that conservation and new development are not automatically in conflict; rather (as schemes at Lewins Mead, Lodge Street and Old Market demonstrate) they frequently can - and should - complement each other.

Today, as we enter a new century, Bristol can take satisfaction in a wave of admirable developments. Thanks to Lottery grants, the long-blighted Canon's Marsh area is being transformed as "Harbourside" with buildings by internationally renowned architects adorning fine new public spaces. A supporting commercial element on the west side of New World Square threatened to be overbearing and monolithic; happily, well-argued objections and weight of public opinion persuaded the city council to refuse permission. The hope must now be that a more sympathetic, finer-grained redevelopment will fill the gap without too much of a hiatus.

Linking Harbourside to the city's historic core (where bars seem to be taking over from banking as the staple commercial activity) is another Lottery-backed scheme, the transformation of The Centre from traffic roundabout into civilised public space; the pedestrian link to Narrow Quay and a restored Queen's Square has already been provided by Pero's Bridge. The big disappointment was, of course, that Behnisch's Harbourside Centre - a dramatic and splendidly imaginative centre for the performing arts in a key waterside location - fell victim to an Arts Council funding crisis.

If Harbourside looks like being a success in urban design terms, the same cannot be said of Temple Quay. This large-scale urban regeneration exercise on derelict land north of Temple Meads Station began under the late unlamented Bristol Development Corporation and continues under English Partnerships. Of most of the office blocks completed so far the best that can be said is that they are undistinguished. Several of them look like semi-detached houses stretched to four or five times normal height. One can only hope that this vertically extrapolated noddy-box model will give way to something more imaginative. The one totally welcome outcome of the BDC's reign at Temple Quay remains Alec French Partnership's delightful (but temporary and moveable) Marketing and Exhibition Centre.

Waterside sites on other stretches of the Floating Harbour have produced some boring, banal developments, but none, I think, that rank as disasters. The standard of recent waterside housing and office schemes has been getting better, and there are signs that this improvement will continue. The more the pity, then, that one scheme widely praised by commentators - Bruges Tozer's proposals for a key site at Wapping Wharf, opposite Harbourside - fell victim to what in my view were the misguided objections of local people and the failure of elected councillors to support real architectural quality. That scheme proposed twin, rather sail-like buildings rising to seven storeys in front of the cliff on which stand the 19th century villas and terraces of Cumberland Road. The residents believed their views and sunlight would be seriously diminished; the architects believed they had succeeded in fitting in the required volume of housing in a way which minimised that loss. The developer, Beaufort Homes, then commissioned designs from another respected practice, Feilden Clegg. The irony is that, while it promises to be a stylish, well-put-together development, this new scheme may well cut out more views and sunlight than Bruges Tozer's "twin peaks".

Finally, a word about a debate that has been a counterpoint to Bristol planning and architecture for most of the last two decades of the 20th century: out-of-town development, particularly in the northern fringe. This has aroused passions which may sometimes lead to criticism, explicit or implied, of architects who design out-of-town buildings. The arguments against out-of-town

development generally are, in my view, unanswerable. They weaken not only city centres but, more seriously, local shopping centres and the communities of which they are the focus; they generate a growth in car use which society cannot hope to cater for; and this is bad for the health both of society and of individual citizens. These arguments have now been recognised by planners, central and local government and even - though somewhat equivocally - by car owners and users.

But a number of big developments - the Cribbs Causeway shopping mall, for instance - got away before central government slammed that particular stable door. Some architects may choose not to compete for out-of-town commissions, but those who do should not be criticised if they strive for optimum results in developments which the planning system has approved. The bigger question is how well the city responds to the challenge of out-of-town: how it adapts and gears itself up to survive the competition.

The signs are hopeful. More and more strangers to Bristol are discovering it as a city of delights: a lively, attractive, welcoming environment for living, working and leisure. Bristolians, too, are increasingly taking pride in their city. But that

should not be an excuse for complacency. Much still needs to be done to improve particular areas and rectify the mistakes of the past. As 1960s and '70s buildings come to be perceived as substandard, redevelopment or radical refurbishment can help to repair a damaged townscape and bring about improvements in the public realm. Conservation by demolition is a technique that is gaining much wider recognition.

So the real Bristol has ample attractions, existing and potential, which those convenient but artificial environments of the northern fringe will always lack. The keys to this are a lively mixture of uses, and places and spaces that are neither swamped by road traffic nor dependent on cars for easy access. Here perhaps lies the biggest challenge: to provide Bristol with frequent, reliable public transport - including perhaps trams, perhaps guided buses - which can offer a credible alternative to the car. We should not be talking as if we can do without cars; rather about providing attractive, practical alternatives for some journeys or parts of journeys. This must include convenient interchange with public transport at the point where car use becomes environmentally unacceptable. Here too architecture and urban design have

It might have been...
Bruges Tozer's scheme
for housing at Wapping
Wharf (see page 7).

their role to play - not least in changing people's perceptions of the city and how we use it.

Thanks and acknowledgements to the very many people and sponsors who helped to make this book possible appear on pages 2 and 133. The biggest thanks must, of course, go to my co-author John Trelawny-Ross. His are the photographs; mine the words, and indeed the selection of buildings, which aimed to include some of the most significant buildings in each decade. John is not to be held responsible for the opinions expressed in the text, but I owe him a big debt of gratitude for all the effort, time, chauffeuring, and knowledge and advice that he has so willingly given to the project.

Tony Aldous, January 2000

1

The first two decades
1900-1919

In Bristol, as elsewhere in Britain, the Edwardian era was a period of prosperity and self-assurance. Solid quality and conservatism were the architectural hallmarks, the results generally solid and uneventful.

A few architects broke out of these constraints, and found clients willing to be more adventurous: two Bristol buildings by Charles Holden illustrate this. Others, like Henry Dare Bryan, worked within the traditional forms yet rose above and transformed them.

1 Former Western Congregational College, 1905-6 now The Family Practice (medical centre)
Henry Dare Bryan

Bryan's Western Congregational College, a theological college for that church, is a beautifully composed building which makes the most of a prominent corner site. Its plan has been described as butterfly-shaped; its main elevation a reworking of Elizabethan or Jacobean motifs - the tall mullioned windows, the almost over-eventful skyline. But whatever else it may be, the design is not slavish. Visually it works.

And functionally, nowadays, the building works for its living by providing a home for a medical practice. The rooms where theological students once lived and worked now provide consulting and treatment rooms of a spaciousness and quality rarely now affordable.

11

2 Former Homeopathic Hospital, 1908/1921
Sir George Oatley

Now a university building, this in some respects echoes its near neighbour, the Western Congregational College - though plainer, more austere and more vertical. This was a delayed project: designed in 1908 but built only in 1921. The north elevation on to Cotham Hill is enlivened by a vigorous little porte-cochère, but it is the southern, downhill elevation that most impresses: a strongly vertical pattern of windows and chimneys; a curving plan with recessed and projecting walls sweeping up from the garden; and triple-arched loggias for patients to take the air and sun. The treatment of the gables is one that Oatley used again at Wills Hall (page 36).

**Former Homeopathic
Hospital** *(2)*
Cotham Hill, BS8
PRESENT OWNER
University of Bristol
ARCHITECT
Sir George Oatley

Central Library *(3)*
College Green,
Bristol, BS1
OWNER
Bristol City Council
ARCHITECT
Charles Holden

3 Central Library, 1906
Charles Holden

Charles Holden (1875-1960) is best known for his 1920s London Underground stations. Two Bristol buildings, designed when he was barely 30, show the path he meant to follow: classical proportion, minimal decoration. The Central Library's front seems to contradict this; but the front, no doubt giving Edwardian city fathers what they thought proper to a major public building, is less than half the story.

Go round to the back, where the ground falls and the building has more storeys, and you have a sense of dèja vu. Uncompromising, unadorned, almost fortress-like, it brings to mind Charles Rennie Mackintosh's Glasgow School of Art, whose construction straddles the library's completion date. So did Holden influence Mackintosh, or vice-versa? Either way Holden's library is, as Dr Timothy Mowl puts it, "a wonderful confidence trick; the kind of modern building a traditionalist feels able to digest".

← **Bristol Royal Infirmary (original building)** *(4)*
Marlborough Hill, Bristol, BS2
OWNER
United Bristol Healthcare Trust
ARCHITECT
Adams & Holden

4 Bristol Royal Infirmary (original building), 1906
Adams & Holden

Holden's Bristol Royal Infirmary, though now all but engulfed by the cuckoo of post-war hospital expansion, is still intact and visible from Marlborough Street, and hints (though with less fluidity of form) at his future London Transport Headquarters of 1929.

Everard's Printing →
Works *(5)*
Broad Street, Bristol, BS1
OWNER
National Westminster plc
ARCHITECT
Henry Williams

5 Everard's Printing Works, 1900
now part of National Westminster Bank
Henry Williams

Undoubtedly Bristol's best and most complete example of art
nouveau, Everard's Printing Works was the product of three
designers: the architect Henry Williams; printer Edward Everard,
client and inspiration for the gorgeous tiled facade; and W J
Neatby, who gave magnificent expression in faience to Everard's
ideas. The key to it all is in the spandrels of the first floor window
arches - the figures of Morris and Gutenberg symbolise the
hoped-for union of industry and art, and might surprise people
who talk as if public art in new buildings was something new.
Now a listed historic building, Everard's was incorporated in 1973
into a NatWest Bank development which commendably retains
this historic area's street pattern and scale.

← **Cabot Café** (6)
38 College Green,
Bristol, BS1
OWNER
City Council
ARCHITECT
LaTrobe & Weston

Jamaica Street →
Carriage Works (7)
Jamaica Street,
Kingsdown, BS2
J L Priest & Co,
ironfounders

6 former Cabot Café, 1900
LaTrobe & Weston

No 38 College Green was, it is said, the best of several art nouveau cafés in Bristol. Now with modern shop front, it is but a fragment of its former self - but for those with the habit of looking above shop fronts, worth more than a glance. Sad that at the time of writing the building seems empty.

7 Jamaica Street Carriage Works, 1905 and 1909
J L Priest & Co

The Jamaica Street carriage works was Bristol's first full-blooded venture into structural cast-iron. The supporting columns are exposed on ground and first floors; on the two top storeys (added 1909) they are encased in brick. Lacking almost all adornment, this building would not, when new, have been regarded as "architecture". Now we may see it as a locally significant piece of early functional design. Still functional, and still in use - though not by carriage-makers.

8 Air Balloon Schools, 1905
LaTrobe & Weston

The Air Balloon Schools are a much more conscious exercise in muscular functionalism - uncompromising in dour grey granite, but relieved by Bath stone dressings and a sometimes playful use of motifs that spring from art nouveau. Chunky but fun. And for more than 90 years, infants and juniors have felt at home here. The local place-name "Air Balloon" celebrates the Montgolfier-inspired ballooning mania of the 1780s, when a Dr Dinwiddie landed his balloon hereabouts after a three-hour flight from Bath.

↑ **Air Balloon Schools** *(8)*
Hillside Road,
St George, BS5
OWNER
Bristol City Council
ARCHITECT
LaTrobe & Weston

The White House *(9)* →
Abbots Leigh Road,
Leigh Woods, BS8
ARCHITECT
Henry Dare Bryan

9 The White House, 1901
Henry Dare Bryan

A number of houses marked the arrival of arts & crafts architecture in Bristol. Bryan's White House, over the Suspension Bridge in arcadian Leigh Woods, has more than a touch of Voysey about it: unadorned, single-colour walls; casement windows ranged horizontally, with opened shutters extending that horizontality; and a balanced but asymmetrical composition, with upward sweeping, double height twin-peaked gables, tall thin chimneys and box dormers, all parts of a skyline at once harmonious and dramatic. Had Bryan perhaps seen Voysey's tower house in London's Bedford Park, built 10 years earlier?

10 42-44 Downs Park East, 1908
Rodway & Dening

Downs Park East and West offer a rich variety of house designs. Nos 42-44 Downs Park East form a beautifully composed semi-detached pair, tile-hung and pitched-roofed for their top two-and-a-half storeys. White-painted, multi-paned casements contrast with the warm red tiles; double-height on the ground floor, horizontal ranges on the upper floors, increased by white-painted panels with lozenges; each window slightly overhung by the tiled facade above.

11 University of Bristol: Old Chemistry Building, 1909
Oatley & Lawrence

This was the first of a whole series of buildings Oatley designed
for the University - or, as it still was when this building was
commissioned, the University College. There was, however, already
a strong tradition of gothic for educational buildings by other
architects: Queen Elizabeth's Hospital (Thomas Foster, 1840s);
Clifton College (Charles Hansom, 1860s); Bristol Grammar
School, on the other side of University Road (Foster & Wood,
1879); and the earliest purpose-built premises for the University
College on the same side as this building (Hansom again, also
1879).

The Chemistry building turns the corner out of University
Road, which makes its main elevation face north-east - so has
large tall windows in its two- and three-storey battlemented bays.
As Andor Gomme points out, there is less decoration, the
stonework is plain, smooth ashlar rather than rubble. The College
(which gained its university charter in the year this building was
completed) presumably liked what it got, and Oatley's emerging
style is to be found in the University Tower (page 27), designed in
1914 though built only after World War I.

**42-44 Downs Park
East** (10)
Westbury Park, BS9
ARCHITECT
Rodway & Dening

Old Chemistry →
Building (11)
University Road,
Clifton, BS8
CLIENT
University of Bristol
ARCHITECT
Oatley & Lawrence

12 Old Bristol Times & Mirror building 1904
Foster & Wood

This delightful example of the arts & crafts movement in Bristol is too little appreciated, probably because it is tucked away in the narrow, northern part of St Stephen Street, invisible from the Centre. On the evidence of its appearance in summer 1999, it could do with some appreciation in the form of a thoroughgoing refurbishment by architects and craftsmen sensitive to its character. Arts & crafts buildings like this, with its three-storey high wooden bays and wealth of ornament, do not just look after themselves. They need loving care. Given it, they can blossom and command the enthusiasm not just of devotees of the movement but of a wider public. Wanted: an owner or occupier who can make that happen.

← **Old Bristol Times &
Mirror** (12)
15-17 St Stephen Street,
City Centre, BS1
CLIENT
Bristol Times & Mirror
ARCHITECT
Foster & Wood

Shirehampton Village ↗
Hall (13)
Station Road,
Shirehampton, BS11
ARCHITECT
F Bligh Bond

B-Bond Warehouse (14) →
Smeaton Road,
Cumberland Basin, BS1
CLIENT
Bristol City Council
BUILDER
Wiliam Cowlin & Sons

13 Shirehampton Village Hall, 1904
F Bligh Bond

Eclectic is a not unfair description of this village hall, now the local public library, by an architect who did much to give the heart of Shirehampton a distinctive character. Its tower and ogee-shaped spire remind one a little of churches in Copenhagen; some of its windows could be Queen Anne; and there are twirly columns which look rather Elizabethan. But it has the organic composition of an arts & crafts building, and it all hangs together in a very jolly, endearing way. Eclecticism with such a lively spirit is not to be sniffed at - it is a building for "Sh'rampt'n" to be proud of and cherish.

14 B-Bond Warehouse, 1908
William Cowlin & Sons

This is one of three apparently identical bonded tobacco warehouses built on either side of the New Cut between 1905 and 1919. Nine storeys high and twice as long, they have a monumental grandeur which derives not just from size but from materials - red brick with a base of blue engineering brick - and the simplicity and rhythm of their main elevations.

In fact the structure of B-bond differs from that of its neighbour to the east, A-Bond. That is steel framed; B-Bond is a pioneering example of concrete frame using the Coignet system with wires as well as tension and compression bars. C-Bond across the river has a similar structure.

B-Bond is owned and part occupied by the city council - at the time of writing the lower floors are split vertically between Bristol Record Office and Create, a project to demonstrate and encourage more environmentally friendly and resource-conserving ways of living. Attached to its eastern end is the Ecohome (see page 106). Further re-use of the upper floors for council activities is planned, but this admirable aim of recycling redundant warehouse space has to overcome the problem of tight headrooms on all but the ground floor: not much more than 1.9m (6ft 6ins). Plenty of people are happy to live in listed country cottages with lower ceilings. Are rules or expectations more demanding for offices?

2

Inter-war years
1920-39

These two decades were a period when Bristol's architecture fought its way out of its historicist past and into the 20th century. Why, then, begin this section with a large chunk of repro gothic? First because Oatley's Wills Memorial and Physics buildings for the University are grand and splendid structures; but also because they illustrate the powerful forces (Wills family patronage, client conservatism, distrust of new techniques) which Modernists in Bristol had to overcome.

**Wills Memorial
Building** *(15)*
Queen's Road,
Clifton, BS8
CLIENT
Sir George Wills
PRESENT OWNER
University of Bristol
ARCHITECT
Sir George Oatley

15 Wills Memorial Building, 1925
Sir George Oatley

The University Tower, dominant at the top of Park Street, has
come to symbolise the pride and ambition of the city as well as its
90-year-old university. The Wills Memorial Building, of which the
tower is part, was the gift of Sir George Wills, head of the Wills
tobacco empire - in those days it was politically correct for
academics to benefit from the profits of what we now recognise as
the carcinogenic weed.

The tower also reminds us that architecture in Bristol is
often about hills: how architects cope with sometimes dramatic
changes in levels and how they exploit (or abuse) an eventful
topography. It may also be taken to symbolise Bristol's attitude to
new buildings. Though a tour de force, it was out of its time - a
last magnificent gasp of 19th-century gothic at a time when 20th-
century functionalism was increasingly gaining acceptance.

16 University Physics Building, 1929
Sir George Oatley

Oatley dreamed of ringing the University's hilltop site with twelve giant gothic towers. He achieved two: at the top of Park Street and here, at Royal Fort. One has mixed feelings. The tower is stylistically backward-looking and has no functional justification; but it is a grand gesture and a splendid feature on the Bristol skyline. And the laboratories behind those absurdly tall windows have such spaciousness, such solidity and quality: 70-year-old wood and metal still looking good for another 70!

↑ **University Physics Building** *(16)*
Royal Fort, Bristol, BS2
OWNER
University of Bristol
ARCHITECT
Sir George Oatley

17 Whiteladies Cinema, 1921
LaTrobe & Weston

Surprising to find that this building - originally conceived as an entertainment complex with cinema, dance hall and restaurant in one building - is four years older than the neo-gothic University Tower. But in the 1920s and '30s it is as if designers of cinemas (which were for their audiences places of escape from a humdrum world) received tacit licence for a romantic eclecticism not granted to other architects. This building is an event in the Whiteladies Road streetscape, recognised with affection by generations of Bristolians.

How sad that the designers of today's generation of multi-screen cinemas (and their clients) seem for the most part content to build nondescript sheds, scarcely distinguishable from the sheds that house light industry or DIY stores. Whiteladies Cinema suffers no such crisis of architectural identity; clustered round it are numerous agreeable places to eat and drink; and you don't need to use your car to get to it.

**Whiteladies →
Cinema** *(17)*
Whiteladies Road,
Clifton, BS8
OWNER
ABC Cinemas
ARCHITECT
LaTrobe & Weston

18 Royal Sun Alliance building
(former Electricity Offices), 1938
Sir Giles Gilbert Scott

A peninsular building thrusting proudly into The Centre, this was designed for a function which scarcely now exists: a prestige development for a public utility combining offices and ground-floor showrooms. Six storeys high and in an alien hard, white Portland stone, it must have seemed to many a boorish intruder alongside the medieval and Georgian buildings of the historic core. But Bristolians have long since first taken it for granted, more recently begun to admire its contribution to a familiar but heterogenous townscape. But then tolerance of neighbours with different styles is relatively recent. According to Tom Burrough, in the late 1930s the Western Chapter of Architects thought the whole city centre should be rebuilt in this style.

Each of the top two storeys is set back from the floor below, which saves it from being overbearing; the curving prow is highly effective, but need floors 1 to 3 of the bow have been set back so deeply, requiring that rather awkward, blank return from the long side elevations instead of curving straight out of them? This is said to be the first Bristol building with a purpose-built underground car park. Scott could scarcely have foreseen that, six decades later, the city's planners would be busily squeezing most cars out of The Centre.

19 Northcliffe House, circa 1929
Ellis & Clarke

Northcliffe House (with its echoes of battles between two evening newspapers, *Post* and *World*) is a piece of unashamed display, a deliberately bold, challenging statement from a newspaper publisher: a series of three-storey verticals containing widows, on either side of a clock-tower set above the main entrance. Surprisingly, it does no real violence to the setting of its neighbour St Mary on the Quay, and remains a valuable element in the varied townscape of The Centre.

↑ **Former Electricity Offices** *(18)*
Colston Avenue, City Centre, BS1

PRESENT OCCUPIER
Royal Sun Alliance
ARCHITECT
Sir Giles Gilbert Scott

↑ **Northcliffe House** *(19)*
Colston Avenue, City Centre, BS1
ARCHITECT
Ellis & Clarke

20 Colston House, 1935
Whinney, Son & Austen Hall

↑ **Colston House** (20)
Colston Street, City
Centre, BS1
OWNER
Bristol City Council
ARCHITECT
Whinney, Son &
Austen Hall

Resolutely "modern", Colston House - which was the Bristol Gas
Company's showrooms and offices and until recently housed the
City Council's information centre - is a beautifully crafted
building, with every detail well considered. Notice particularly the
projecting central bay at first and second floor level with curved
corners to its horizontal line of windows, and the way the building
turns the corner into Pipe Lane.

21 The Concrete House, 1934
Connell & Ward

Amyas Connell pioneered functionalist, modern house design in Britain, provoking both praise and derision with his 1929 High & Over at Amersham, Buckinghamshire. He then teamed up with Basil Ward for a series of houses, including this one. Common characteristics of the new approach, practised by several other architects including Maxwell Fry, include (1) rational rather than symmetrical floor plan; (2) unadorned rendered or concrete walls; (3) flat roofs; and (4) horizontal strips of glazing allied with (5) orientation to maximise sunlight. The uncompromisingly named Concrete House has all these, plus a three-storey glass and metal-framed stair tower giving access to a sun-roof. Its severely rectilinear lines are relieved by a curving entrance porch. Well cared for by appreciative owner-occupiers.

The Concrete ↑
House (21)
← The Ridgeway,
Westbury-on-Trym, BS10
ARCHITECT
Connell & Ward

22 The Council House, 1938
E Vincent Harris

The Council ↗
House *(22)*
College Green,
Bristol, BS1
OWNER
Bristol City Council
ARCHITECT
E Vincent Harris

In contrast to the enlightened private patronage and forward-looking architecture of the Concrete House is the city council's big prestige project of the '30s: its headquarters, the Council House. Its virtues are its curving plan and two giant book-end portes-cochères, but the overall impression it leaves is of extrapolated neo-Georgian in which repeat fenestration fails to match scale. Brick as the main material does not help. It ends up looking boring.

Public spaces inside have presence without being overbearing. The golden unicorns on the roof scandalised Bristolians at the time (what a waste of public money!). Bristol now appreciates the way they enliven the skyline. The real scandal was the way the architect was chosen. The then President of the Royal Institute of British Architects, Vincent Harris, judged an architectural competition, found none of the entries worthy, and offered to do the job himself. These days both the RIBA and Bristol do things more correctly.

23 St Monica Home of Rest, 1928
Sir George Oatley

If the Wills family's preferred architectural style was more than a little passé by the late 1920s, in the hands of Oatley it provided Bristol with some marvellously romantic skylines. St Monica's - in landscaped grounds almost merging with the wide expanse of Durdham Down - is a relaxed arrangement of three- and four-storey buildings broken by three-storey Tudor bays with timber gables or battlements, and with soaring triple Tudor chimneys. It was conceived by Dame Monica Wills as a well-endowed retirement home where professional people handicapped by illness could live comfortable and well-cared-for lives, and that function it has continued and developed.

For all its neo-Elizabethan style, St Monica's demonstrates Oatley's skill in functional design. The main building groups individual rooms and flats round common "family unit" facilities, just as Bengough House (page 113) does 70 years later. He gives it spacious, accessible balconies and orientation makes the most of sunshine. Of course there have been alterations and additions, generally tactfully done. One which might with benefit be adopted in much more modern institutional buildings is the fitting of sensors to doors into the garden to allow wheelchair-bound residents to come and go as they please.

24 St Edyth's Church, 1928
Sir George Oatley

St Edyth's stands at a corner of The Pentagon, a five-armed cross-roads presumably aimed at providing a focal point for an estate of decent but unexciting inter-war terrace housing. The church is one of Oatley's late gothic buildings, but a very restrained gothic with little ornament; the setting did not call for it and the budget no doubt forebade it. Indeed building was left incomplete for another 70 years. But it is skilfully and harmoniously put together, and the 1990s addition by Peter Ware - providing two church halls plus meeting rooms - is sympathetically done.

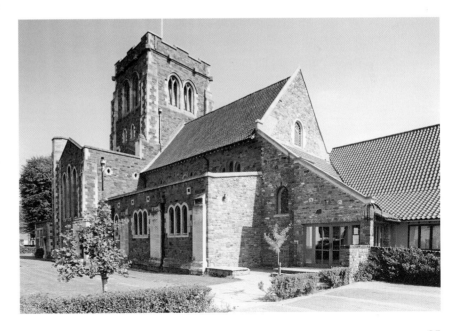

↖ **St Monica Home of Rest** (23)
Cote Lane,
Westbury-on-Trym, BS9
OWNER
St Monica Home of Rest
ARCHITECT
Sir George Oatley

St Edyth's →
Church (24)
The Pentagon,
Sea Mills, BS9
OWNER
Church Of England
ARCHITECT
Sir George Oatley

↑ **Wills Hall** *(25)*
Parry's Lane, Stoke
Bishop, BS9
OWNER
University of Bristol
ARCHITECT
Sir George Oatley

25 Wills Hall, 1925
Sir George Oatley

Another Oatley building on the northern edge of Durdham Down, Wills Hall continues the "tobacco gothic" demanded by the Wills family, but in a sparer, cleaner form. It was the University's first purpose-built men's hall of residence, and followed an abortive proposal that Goldney House should serve that purpose. The then warden of a neighbouring women's hall, Clifton Hill House, was appalled at the prospect of male undergraduates living in such close proximity to "her gels" and threatened to resign. Sir George Wills was CHH's treasurer and supported her stand, so presumably felt an obligation to provide an alternative. The result: what Andor Gomme has called "a closed quadrangle of Cotswold Elizabethan ... with rows of large gables inside and out, like a cross between a manor house and an Oxford college."

The present writer has, as a former Wills student, some difficulty in treating this building objectively. If utility, durability and delight are the three hallmarks of successful architecture, in some measure it provides all three. It is full of character, like other Wills benefactions marvellously well built, and the accommodation is spacious even if not wheelchair-accessible. Post-war extensions include a discreetly sited but utilitarian L-shaped block by Oatley partner Ralph Brentnall, a second L-shaped block to complete a new, more open quadrangle, and an adjoining conference hall. The 28-acre site provided by the Wills family now accommodates three further halls of residence: Churchill, Badock and Hiatt Baker. All are, of course, these days mixed-gender.

26 Fresco Italian Brasserie, 1935
A W Roques, Sir Giles Gilbert Scott

Built as a bank with offices above, like so many others in Corn Street, this tall narrow frontage generally escaped notice until its recent refurbishment and its new use as a restaurant made passers-by aware of its stylishness and joie de vivre. The frontage, which is Gilbert Scott's part of the job, is in a stripped classical style, but nonetheless has its own distinctive character, and cleaning has spotlighted jolly details including the rather Gill-like relief carvings by Hermon Cawthra and its tall, very French-looking windows.

Corn Street is a rich street architecturally, and there is no reason why the departure of banks should be bad for it. Restaurants and bars bring a different kind of vitality, and, one hopes, the money to keep these buildings in the style to which they ought to be accustomed.

Fresco Italian →
Brasserie *(26)*
No 37 Corn Street, City
Centre, BS1
ARCHITECTS
A W Roques; Sir Giles
Gilbert Scott
SCULPTOR
Hermon Cawthra

3

Brave new world
1940-59

This was a thin time for architecture in Bristol. Even when World War II ended in 1945, shortage and rationing of building materials curtailed the scope for new buildings of quality; and in the '50s, stylistic conservatism still for the most part ruled. Some of the most adventurous buildings, in Bristol as elsewhere in Britain, came from public sector architects, inspired both by the ideal of a better world for ordinary people and by the new functionalism.

27 City Council Flats, Redcliffe, 1950+
Bristol City Architect's Department

Redcliffe Flats *(27)*
Commercial Road,
Redcliffe, BS1
CLIENT
Bristol City Council
ARCHITECT
Bristol City Architect's
Department

Perhaps these flats, overlooking the muddy waters of The Cut at Redcliffe, owed something to an enthusiasm for Corbusier of some lively spirit in the City Architect's Department. High-rise slabs and towers soon afterwards became unpopular in Britain. Yet if well built, in the right place, with an appropriate and willing tenant mix and good management, they can work well. Inner city Redcliffe was the right place. And as far as looks go, they are still a strong, attractive piece of townscape.

28 Former Lewis's Department Store, 1957
now Bentall's
Sir Percy Thomas & Son

Two prestigious late 1950s building projects for Bristol, one public sector, one private. The private-sector scheme, for Lewis's department store, was down in the city centre where a heavily bombed Bristol had relocated its post-war shopping. The site was tight, awkwardly shaped, and steeply sloping. The architects overcame these difficulties and produced a landmark building whose 6-storey rounded "prow" exploits its location. Forward-looking for its day, yet with popular appeal.

29 Queen's Building, 1958
Oatley & Brentnall

The public project was new engineering, medical and mathematics buildings for Bristol's growing university. Its hilltop site is magnificent and, from a distance, its skyline wall of buildings has a certain grandeur. Ralph Brentnall, Oatley's partner and survivor, copes reasonably well with the site's steep slope. But, whether from loss of nerve or lack of money, Brentnall's Queen's Building appears today a timid compromise: token classical detail makes it look a leftover from Oatley, for instance, instead of something more robustly of its age.

↑ **Queen's Building** (29)
University Walk, BS8
CLIENT
University of Bristol
ARCHITECT
Oatley & Brentnall
QUANTITY SURVEYOR
Bernard & Son
STRUCTURAL ENGINEER
Mouchell & Partners
MECHANICAL ENGINEER
G N Haden
ELECTRICAL ENGINEER
W T Porter
MAIN CONTRACTOR
William Cowlin & Sons

← **Lewis's department store** (28)
The Horsefair, BS1
ORIGINAL CLIENT
Lewis Ltd
PRESENT OWNER
Bentalls
ARCHITECT
Sir Percy Thomas & Son
STRUCTURAL ENGINEER
W J Jones, Liverpool
MECHANICAL AND
ELECTRICAL ENGINEER
O C Waygood, Liverpool

QUANTITY SURVEYOR
W T Hills & Co, Cardiff
LANDSCAPE ARCHITECT
Sudell & Waters, London
MAIN CONTRACTOR
John Morgan (Builders)
Ltd, Cardiff
1998 CLIENT
Bentalls
ARCHITECTS FOR
REFURBISHMENT
Stride Treglown Ltd

30 Brabazon Assembly Hall, 1949
Eric Ross

In the late 1940s, in a time of still acute post-war shortages, the then Bristol Aeroplane Company launched, with government funding, an ambitious project to build a super airliner: the Brabazon. To assemble it they needed a very large shed - to move the completed aircraft out called for continuous sliding doors the whole width of the building: some 320m. The height - 36m - means that the building still dominates the Filton skyline, even in the context of the much expanded British Aerospace Airbus complex.

The building's structure was innovative. On the steel frame was fitted a light weight, "dry in construction", cladding consisting of prefabricated panels of asbestos cement; the steel-deck roof has a single impervious covering. Clerestoreys and a full-width glazed wall at the opposite end from the sliding doors ensured good working conditions. A boiler house, canteen, and storage for inflammable materials were built alongside. In all sorts of ways the Assembly Hall pioneered new approaches and techniques followed as a matter of course in later industrial buildings.

31 Lockleaze Secondary School, 1954+
Bristol City Architect's Department

The 1944 Butler Education Act led - once the resources were available - to a greatly expanded programme of school building which traditional construction methods could not meet quickly or cheaply enough. In the late 1950s and '60s various systems of prefabricated construction came to the rescue, the best known being CLASP. Lockleaze - with its pre-cast concrete frame, walls with brick infill panels, and pre-stressed concrete floors — was a pioneer in this kind of modular construction. Since then the building has been much added to and modified to meet today's requirements, for instance in respect of security, but the clean lines and basic form of the original can still be appreciated and - according to staff - it still performs well as a school.

Brabazon Assembly Hall *(30)*
Filton, BS12
CLIENT
Bristol Aeroplane Co
ARCHITECT
BAC Architect (Eric Ross)

Lockleaze Secondary School *(31)* →
Hogarth Walk,
Lockleaze, BS7
CLIENT
Bristol City Council
ARCHITECT
City Architect's
Department

4

Swinging sixties
1960-69

The 1960s were when Bristol began rediscovering modern architecture, but wasn't quite sure if it liked it. Getting away from tired old styles depended on enthusiastic architects finding patrons who shared their vision, or thought the new look prestigious. Span houses in Sneyd Park were unlike any built in post-war Bristol; Bristol Water went boldly for an international-style headquarters; Anglican and Catholic churches were nudged into breaking the architectural mould; and a new shot tower, in unashamedly naked concrete, broke the city skyline.

One Redcliff St (32)
Bristol, BS1
CLIENT
E S & A Robinson
Holdings Ltd
ARCHITECT
DRG Architects
QUANTITY SURVEYOR
E T Wraight, Bristol
STRUCTURAL ENGINEER
Sir Robert McAlpine,
London
MECHANICAL AND
ELECTRICAL ENGINEERS
Hayden, Bristol; G
Granek, Toronto
MAIN CONTRACTOR
Sir Robert McAlpine,
Newport

32 One Redcliff Street, 1964
DRG Architects

This building shows what resulted when one of Bristol's leading
companies, paper-makers E S & A Robinson, encouraged its in-
house architects department to design a austerely simple tower in
the manner of Mies van der Rohe as its headquarters near Bristol
Bridge. In many ways No 1 Redcliff Street - bold, clean-lined and
well detailed - marked Bristol's arrival in the world of 1960s architecture. It was a superb landmark when the Bristol skyline was
lower, but still looks good. Its designers took on their own identity
as Group Architects DRG, later incorporated into another leading
Bristol practice, BGP.

33 Shot Tower, 1968
E N Underwood & Partners

It was in 1728 in a house on Bristol's Redcliffe Hill that William Watts perfected the manufacture of lead shot for muskets by pouring molten lead from a great height into water. When shot-making was transferred to Cheese Lane in the 1960s, the company commissioned this very 1960-ish, but beautiful, concrete shot tower from consulting engineers Underwood. It went out of use a decade ago but is now "listed" and protected from demolition. A popular and important feature of the city skyline.

← **Shot Tower** *(33)*
Cheese Lane, BS2
CLIENT
Sheldon Bush & Patent
Shot Co
DESIGNER
E N Underwood &
Partners
QUANTITY SURVEYOR
Banks Wood & Partners

34 Bristol Water head office, 1963
Watkins Gray & Partners

In the '60s a government policy of rationalising the water industry led to Bristol Water taking over numerous local water undertakings. The enlarged company needed new offices, and commissioned a boldly modern headquarters on surplus waterworks land at Bedminster Down. Looking like concrete but in fact clad in tiles, it is very much a '60s building. Clean-lined and low, it skilfully conceals considerable bulk. Right for its site, but in the end rather anonymous.

35 Manor Park Estate, 1959 onwards
Whicheloe Macfarlane Architects

The Manor Park Estate was Whicheloe Macfarlane's admirable bid to show that suburban need not mean subtopian. They were fortunate in their client - a local firm of builder developers - who believed quality mattered, including quality of the outside environment. Developed over a decade, Manor Park has two elements: two-storey terraces made lively by a well-chosen palette of materials and indentation of elevations; and rather restrained, crisply detailed three-storey blocks of flats. All in agreeable landscaped setting with the impact of cars minimised.

↑ **Bristol Water** *(34)*
Bridgwater Road, BS13
CLIENT
Bristol Waterworks Company
ARCHITECT
Watkins Gray & Partners

STRUCTURAL ENGINEER
Clarke Nichols & Marcel
MAIN CONTRACTOR
Costain Construction

Manor Park →
Estate *(35)*
Malmains Drive,
Frenchay, BS16
CLIENT AND BUILDER
W & D Malpass, Bristol
ARCHITECT, PLANNERS,
LANDSCAPE ARCHITECTS,
STRUCTURAL DESIGNERS
Whicheloe Macfarlane
Architects

36 Span housing, 1965
Towning Hill & Partners

↑ **Pitch & Pay** *(36)*
Pitch & Pay Lane,
Sneyd Park, BS9
CLIENT
Span Developments
ARCHITECT
Towning Hill & Partners
LANDSCAPE ARCHITECT
Prebend Jakobsen

At about the same time as the Manor Park Estate, an enlightened London-based developer, Span, had been demonstrating that relatively high density, low-rise housing could provide good homes for young professionals - and could sell. The formula included lush existing and new landscape and resident control of maintenance. Span spread from London to other cities, including Bristol, where Towning Hill fitted their development into a hillside site alongside the ancient Roman track to Sea Mills. Their Span designs speak with a distinctive Bristol accent; Pitch & Pay is still a delight.

37 All Saints Church, 1967
Potter & Hare

Here and overleaf are two 1960s churches: one Anglican, the other Catholic; one largely a replacement of a mostly Victorian building, the other a new church to serve new housing estates in south Bristol.

The 19th-century All Saints by G E Street was fatally damaged by incendiary bombs in 1940. The new church incorporates the tower and some other survivals, but externally its outstanding feature is the aluminium-clad, laminated timber spire; on either side of it nave elevations with striking vertical fenestration and reverse pitch roofs. The interior is all light and colour with windows by John Piper and translucent glazing between nave and atrium.

All Saints (37) →
Alma Vale
Road,
Clifton, BS8
CLIENT AND OWNER
Church of England
ARCHITECT
Potter & Hare

← **St Bernadette's** *(38)*
Wells Road,
Whitchurch, BS14
CLIENT AND OWNER
Roman Catholic Diocese
of Clifton
ARCHITECT
Kenneth Nealon Tanner
& Partners
QUANTITY SURVEYOR
Banks Wood & Partners

↙ **Senate House** *(39)*
Tyndall Avenue,
Clifton, BS8
CLIENT
University of Bristol
ARCHITECT
Oatley & Brentnall
QUANTITY SURVEYOR
Bernard & Son
STRUCTURAL ENGINEER
Mouchell & Partners
MAIN CONTRACTOR
Laing

38 St Bernadette's RC Church, 1968
Kenneth Nealon Tanner & Partners

St Bernadette's, with its sail-like roof and triangular glazed fin
sweeping up to a cross, brought visual quality and excitement to this
distinctly unexciting suburb. It still does, despite barbed wire erected
to keep local youth from skateboarding dangerously on the roof.
Indirect natural lighting gives the interior a comfortably tranquil feel.

39 University of Bristol Senate House, 1962
Oatley & Brentnall

The Senate House is a curious building, full of unresolved contradic-
tions. In the years when the Wills family were in effect the clients and
paymasters for the University's buildings, if a senate house had been
deemed necessary it would surely have been a landmark building of
imposing presence. In the early 1960s, neither the money nor the will
to make such a bold statement seem to have existed.

It also looks as though Brentnall was trying to break through
into a new and more functional style: not here the stuck-on
decorative motif of the Queen's Building, but a potentially elegant
grouping of unadorned, angular shapes to house what is after all an
administrative building. But somehow it doesn't quite come off.
Function and form don't by any means tally - in particular, why is the
front door not at the front? Tucking it round the side in Tyndall
Avenue deprives the Woodland Road elevation of the focal point and
activity that could have made it succeed visually. If we wanted to be
kind, we could say that this was, both for the University and
Brentnall, a time of transition - but, alas, they hadn't quite got there.

40 Library, Badminton School, 1969
Casson Conder & Partners

Library, ↑
Badminton
School *(40)*
Westbury Road,
Westbury-on-Trym, BS9
CLIENT
Governors of Badminton
School
ARCHITECT
Casson Conder
& Partners

Badminton School, an independent school for girls, occupied a large old house set in landscaped gardens of some historical importance. In the 1960s this building became inadequate, and the school has added several others - library, sixth-form centre, music school, art centre - always striving to obtain buildings which not only met functional needs but looked good in the landscape. Casson Conder's library was the first, and perhaps set

the marker for quality.

It is essentially a garden pavilion, two storeys high, sited at the corner of a raised terrace. The upper storey, which is the reading room, looks out on that level. Externally the building is a cool, simple, white cube with grey pitched roof. The reading room, focusing round stairhead and librarian's desk, must be a good place to study. It can scarcely, of course, meet current criteria for a modern, computerised library, but that is hindsight. As a building which enhances rather than damages an important setting, it still merits study - and admiration.

5

The rise of conservation
1970-79

In the 1960s and early '70s, Bristol - like not a few other British cities - sold its architectural soul for a mess of pottage. Much that was historic, much that had to do with the grain and spirit of the place, was swept away to make room for big, ungainly and supposedly functional buildings. Speculative office development wrecked the Rupert Street/Lewins Mead area; hospital and university development severely damaged the slopes of the Georgian suburb of Kingsdown. The graceful Georgian houses were run-down, ergo they had to go.

The later 1970s were a time of fight-back. The approach to European Architectural Heritage Year, 1975, threw a spotlight on the alternative approach: repair, conserve, reinforce by infill. At Lodge Street and Old Market, buildings written off as beyond repair were rescued and turned to new or adapted uses. The small-scale grain of well-loved historic areas was preserved; developers and their clients came to see that adaptive re-use of attractive and unusual buildings gave a certain cachet to real estate. Much had been lost - but that made what remained all the more worth striving to keep.

41 Inner city repair and renewal c1978-1985
Ferguson Mann Architects

The steeply sloping Lodge Street/Trenchard Street site just west of the city centre contained empty and deteriorating 18th- and 19th-century houses and an 18th-century chapel. A developer proposed demolition for offices. The city council urged housing; a public

inquiry upheld this view; and a housing association bought the site. Ferguson Mann rescued the shells of 11 Georgian houses and the chapel and inserted new flats and houses into them. Other ingredients include new housing at the top of the site, landscaped central garden, a pedestrian route running through and under buildings.

The client also acquired The Presbytery, an 18th-century building previously occupied by Jesuit priests; this was converted into five flats, and its garden, with mulberry tree, was used to extend the attractive sequence of landscaped spaces. The scheme - crucially assisted by national and city council conservation grants - yielded altogether 56 homes. It has proved popular with tenants and has been a major factor in bringing life back into central Bristol.

**Repair and renewal
at Lodge Street** (41)
Lodge Street, BS1
CLIENT
Bristol Churches Housing
Association
ARCHITECT
Ferguson Mann
Architects
QUANTITY SURVEYOR
Gleeds
STRUCTURAL
ENGINEER
Mander Raikes &
Marshall
LANDSCAPE
ARCHITECT
Ferguson Mann
Architects
MAIN CONTRACTOR
John Laing

42 Old Market: conservation and renewal, 1977 onwards
Peter Ware, Ferguson Mann, Leonard Mannesseh
Partnership

In the 1950s and '60s, Bristol's chief planning officers were engineers; their approach was all too often to clear decaying but attractive old buildings to make way for roads and bigger, less attractive new buildings. From the mid-'70s, the city had the benefit of a new breed of city planners, who looked with an architect's eye and saw, not slums, but old buildings and townscape worth keeping and capable of refurbishment.

Old Market is one of the city's most historic areas, but it was severed from the centre by a new super-highway, and suffered grievously from blight and decay. Its rescue has been slow, achieved against the odds, and is still to be completed. It has been accomplished by a partnership of planners, conservationists, property owners and architects and builders; and, paradoxically, selective demolition and new build have been a prerequisite of saving the frontage buildings. The Historic Buildings Council and its successor English Heritage played a key role: giving official, national authority to the notion that these buildings were worth saving, and providing essential matching funding. The work continues.

**Old Market:
conservation and
renewal** *(42)*
Old Market, BS2
CLIENT AND OWNER
Bristol City Council,
Bristol Municipal
Charities and others
ARCHITECTS
Peter Ware, Ferguson
Mann, Leonard
Mannesseh Partnership,
and others.

43 High Kingsdown, 1974
Whicheloe & Macfarlane

Two very different attempts to get away from unsatisfactory forms of development. High Kingsdown was in part a reaction against the blockbuster hospital and housing schemes which had wrecked the lower slopes of Kingsdown. Bristol Civic Society campaigned against more of the same, and the city council (the landowner) relented. The scheme does have one multi-storey slab, unobtrusively sited near St Michael's Hill. The rest of the development is two-storey houses in yellow brick, served by paved pedestrian lanes. It provides an attractive human-scale environment, and brought fresh life and hope to what was a decaying inner city neighbourhood.

44 Five Houses, Flax Bourton, 1973
Artist Constructor

This group of five houses at Flax Bourton aimed to show that clean modern design could enhance rather than damage a Somerset village. In this the designers Bob Organ (artist) and Tim Organ (builder) succeeded. The houses now have less distinguished neighbours, and most have been altered, but enough remains to indicate the quality of the original concept.

← **High Kingsdown concept design and planning** *(43)*
↙ off St Michael's Hill, Kingsdown, BS2
CLIENT
Bristol City Council, Director of Housing
ARCHITECT AND PROFESSIONAL TEAM
Whicheloe & Macfarlane
COMMERCIAL CONSULTANT
Pritchards, Bristol
DETAILED DESIGN AND PROJECT MANAGEMENT CLIENT
JT Group Limited, Bristol
EXECUTIVE ARCHITECT AND PROFESSIONAL TEAM
JT Building Group
MAIN CONTRACTOR
JT Building Service Ltd

Flax Bourton →
houses *(44)*
Post Office Lane, Flax Bourton, BS48
DEVELOPER AND DESIGNER
Artist Constructor
MAIN CONTRACTOR
direct labour

45 Bristol United Press, 1972
Group Architects DRG

The Bristol United Press building comes of a different world from today's: a world of brutal urban surgery. The design had to cope with the noise, visual intrusion and urban severance of a barbarous inner relief road. The client wanted a highly visible, prestige building to house newspaper presses and offices. Its architects gave it an elegant fortress in purple glazed brick, with cylindrical stair tower, curving corners, and all the solidity and confidence of a medieval keep. Its form enfolds and expresses function. Externally it is not a sociable building - blank walls, not doors and windows - but its setting was not sociable. It rises above that hostile environment, has performed well and still looks well.

↑ **Bristol United Press** *(45)*
   Temple Way, BS2
← **CLIENT**
   Bristol United Press
   ARCHITECTS
   Group Architects DRG
   ENGINEER
   J F Farquharson & Partners
   QUANTITY SURVEYOR
   E T Wraight & Co
   MAIN CONTRACTOR
   Bovis Construction

46 Scottish Life Building, 1976
Group Architects DRG

Just to the south of the BUP building, the same architects designed an office building for Scottish Life, currently occupied by IBM and Guardian Royal. Well composed and clad in tinted glass, it also defies the noise and visual anarchy of the ring-road, but is externally unwelcoming. Its curtain walling has dated less than in many '70s buildings.

Scottish Life →
Building *(46)*
Temple Way, BS2
CLIENT
Scottish Life Association
ARCHITECT
Group Architects DRG
ENGINEER
J F Farquharson &
Partners
QUANTITY SURVEYOR
L C Wakeman &
Partners
MAIN CONTRACTOR
Henry Boot Construction

47 Clifton Cathedral, 1974
Percy Thomas & Son

When the Roman Catholic Cathedral of SS Peter and Paul first appeared among the leafy streets of Georgian and Victorian Clifton, many people resented what they perceived as an out-of-scale, unsympathetic intrusion. Now, after 25 years, they are used to it and feel considerable affection for its triple-bladed spire, whose distant views are as memorable as those in Salisbury or Norwich. Closer external views are of a grey, rough pre-cast cladding which has now toned in with the colours and textures of 19th-century Clifton - and which was the best a not-too-well-heeled diocese could afford.

But it is the interior which worshippers and concert-goers will surely most remember: spacious (1000 people can gather round the central altar), light, and tranquil. The building is an elongated hexagon with a lantern above the high altar rising into the spire. And here the concrete is laid in situ and is very beautiful. Quality control had three standards: high up - not too fussy; clearly visible - must be good; and where you could touch it - perfection. The underground car park - insisted on by 1970s planners - is still ugly. What about some camouflage planting?

Clifton Cathedral *(47)*
Pembroke Road, BS8
CLIENT AND OWNER
The Roman Catholic
Diocese of Clifton
ARCHITECT
Percy Thomas & Son
QUANTITY SURVEYOR
I E Symons & Partners
ENGINEER
Felix Samuely & Partners
ENVIRONMENTAL CONTROL
Engineering Design
Consultants
MAIN CONTRACTOR
John Laing Construction
Limited

48 Colston Centre, 1973
Moxley Jenner & Partners

This is a 1970s building which has aged remarkably well. Despite some 1990s alterations, including a welcome public clock, it still stands with its elegantly detailed white tower rising effortlessly above a long podium, its curved prow solving the problem of a site awkwardly constrained between Colston Avenue and Colston Street. The tower's one fault is that it destroys the illusion of nearby Orchard Street as an intact 18th- century enclave; but from the Centre it seemed to stand as a beacon of hope to Bristolians that eventually order might prevail over the chaos and squalor of that barbaric traffic maelstrom.

And now that traffic is being reduced and subdued there, the Colston tower still stands as a marker of urbane, high quality design - in contrast to that other tower, raised in 1968 by the Bristol and West. That company is, of course, moving to new quarters at Temple Quay. Its old home ought to be demolished: it is too reminiscent of an age of brutalist architecture and pedestrians exiled from the streets to weather-exposed high-level walkways. More probably it will have a new life, perhaps as student flats. Its 17 storeys certainly need recladding - and whoever does the job might do worse than look at the Colston Centre.

← **Colston Centre** *(48)*
Colston Avenue, City
Centre, BS1
CLIENT
Sir Robert McAlpine Ltd
ARCHITECT
Moxley Jenner &
Partners
OTHER CONSULTANTS
Sir Robert McAlpine
CONTRACTOR
Sir Robert McAlpine

49 Wills Hartcliffe, 1977
Skidmore Owings Merrill, YRM

The Wills headquarters and cigarette-making complex at Hartcliffe was criticised when it was built for pulling 1400 people out of the company's traditional heartland, Bedminster, into a suburban location. Hartcliffe was difficult of access for those without cars and short on local facilities, while to the economic and social fabric of inner city Bedminster the move was like a savage kick in the teeth. But from a more narrowly architectural viewpoint, judgments were different. Imperial Tobacco engaged celebrated international architects to design the best, most functional, most prestigious buildings money could buy. As architecture, Wills Hartcliffe was magnificent.

"Was" because, little more than two decades later, this purpose-built, prestige development was empty, and the giant factory building in course of demolition. It was a splendid building: clad in Corten steel, which rusts beautifully (and intentionally); an envelope engineered to accommodate very precisely the needs of 1970s cigarette manufacture; the whole overtopped dramatically by the building's huge steel frame. "King Tobacco's colossal palace," I wrote at the time, perhaps "the grandest shed in Europe".

The office block will presumably escape demolition. It, too, was a beautiful building, set just below the factory and above a delightfully landscaped lake (needed in case of fire); its steel frame standing a metre of so in front of the bronze curtain walling; and staff restaurant and offices opening on to landscaped courtyards. Employees transported from Bedminster's utilitarian red brick must have felt they had made a good exchange. Few of them could have dreamed that it would all so soon become redundant - a 20-year dinosaur. The office block deserves a new lease of life - some company's elegant head office, perhaps.

In August 1999 proposals were published for a large-scale development including a hotel, a DIY store and other shopping, as well as refurbishment of the existing office building. Refurbishment would be welcome, but any new development should be required to respect that building's quality and setting.

Wills Hartcliffe (49)
Hengrove Way,
Hartcliffe, BS13
CLIENT
Imperial Tobacco
ARCHITECT
Skidmore Owings Merrill
EXECUTIVE ARCHITECT
YRM
QUANTITY SURVEYOR
Gleeds, Nottingham
STRUCTURAL ENGINEER
F J Samuely & Partners
MECHANICAL AND
ELECTRICAL CONSULTANT
Steensen Varming
Mulcahy
CONTRACT MANAGEMENT
John Laing Construction

50 Wessex House, 1976
BGP Group Architects

Commissioned by a newly created Wessex Water Authority as its offices and 24-hour control centre, this building comes 13 years after Bristol Water's headquarters on Bedminster Down (page 47) and reflects both its time and the difference of a city centre location. No curtain walled "International" style here. The site itself was not the easiest. The harbour wall was in disrepair; there were rights of light to the adjoining Sheldon Bush (shot tower) premises; and the city council wanted a riverside walk built into the scheme. There was also a certain political sensitivity about what was in fact the new authority's headquarters.

The result is a low, solid-looking, rather chunky building clad mostly in a warm red brick but with tiles to the central core, and with double-glazed windows fitted directly into the brickwork. Its overall character conveys the control centre rather than the head office use. Structurally, it has a reinforced concrete frame on 13-metre deep piles; the lower ground floor contains 28 car spaces. It has a cheerful, robust character and fits well into the Bristol waterside. Only a pity that its waterside walkway comes to an abrupt halt with the neighbouring site. We need a determined push to get it extended towards Temple Meads.

← **Wessex House** (50)
Passage Street, City Centre, BS2
CLIENT
Wessex Water Authority
ARCHITECT
BGP Group Architects
QUANTITY SURVEYOR
Gleeds
STRUCTURAL ENGINEER
L G Mouchel & Partners
MECHANICAL AND ELECTRICAL CONSULTANT
Parsons Brown
LANDSCAPE ARCHITECT
BGP Group Architects
MAIN CONTRACTOR
William Cowlin & Sons Ltd

51 The Pavilions (formerly CEGB SW Region headquarters), 1978
Arup Associates

This was another prestige, purpose-built headquarters which, within a couple of decades, outlived the purpose and organisation that commissioned it. The Central Electricity Generating Board (since split up and privatised) wanted a state-of-the-art headquarters for its south-western region, which stretched from Pembroke to west London. The brief called for a building to contain offices, scientific services, workshops, computer services, a telecommunications centre, restaurant, and sports and social club. It was to be low-energy, making maximum use of natural energy sources and the heat produced by people and machines. It was to accommodate 1200 staff brought together from 14 locations, and required 700 parking spaces.

So a pretty huge building: hence a low horizontal profile to reduce its impact on the Bedminster Down landscape: one and two storeys with shallow-pitched roofs and deeply overhanging eaves. The offices are grouped in seven pavilions (hence the present name) round landscaped courtyards, with a central "street" running from the main entrance to connect with office areas, laboratories, restaurant and social facilities. This is a concept which has since been widely used and adapted: MOD Abbey Wood (page 89) is a recent local example. That the building has proved adaptable is shown by its surviving the demise of the CEGB. At the time of writing, most of the seven pavilions were let to well-established, high-profile firms: the building had proved flexible enough to be sub-divided in this way, with all of them seemingly happy to use high quality common facilities like the restaurant. If this is a dinosaur, it has proved remarkably adaptable.

The Pavilions →
(formerly CEGB) *(51)*
Bedminster Down, BS13
CLIENT
Central Electricity
Generating Board
ARCHITECTS
Arup Associates
ENGINEERING CONSULTANT
Arup Associates
QUANTITY SURVEYOR
Arup Associates
LANDSCAPE ARCHITECT
Peter Swann Associates
MAIN CONTRACTOR
Laing Management
Contracting

6

Urban repair
and improvement
1980-89

In the 1960s and '70s large-scale development - commercial and institutional - had torn much of the heart out of Bristol. Between The Centre and Broadmead, a series of lumpish office blocks linked by never-to-be-completed high-level walkways created an urban wilderness, sterilised by traffic and poisoned by traffic fumes. In the '80s a string of more enlightened developments began the repair of the urban environment: developments which rescued, recreated and reconnected old streets and buildings; created new places and spaces for people on foot; and injected much-needed architectural joie de vivre into a drab and over-bearing business district.

Much of the credit for urban repair, improvement and conservation in the last two decades of the 20th century must go the staff of the city planning department. Everyone loves to blame "the planners", frequently for failures that have nothing to do with the town planning process. Development control officers are seen either as obstructive (when they say No) or pusillanimous (when they fail to say No). The public are seldom aware of the positive, enabling role of planning officers in suggesting ways forward, hammering out compromises, improving poor development proposals and bringing together the parties where a jigsaw of land ownerships requires joint action.

Bristol has been fortunate to have in its planning department architects and design officers who not only possessed the skills - in both design and diplomacy - to make these things happen, but cared greatly about the outcome. It is easy to criticise compromise; the answer to such criticism is often, You should have seen what we'd have got without it. Creative compromise at its best is an art too little celebrated.

52 One Bridewell Street, 1987
Alec French Partnership

One Bridewell Street (52)
Bridewell Street, Bristol, BS1
CLIENT
MEPC for Ernst & Young
ARCHITECT
Alec French Partnership
STRUCTURAL ENGINEER
Clarke Bond Partnership, Bristol
MECHANICAL AND ELECTRICAL
CONSULTANT
W S Atkins & Partners, Bristol
QUANTITY SURVEYOR
Banks Wood & Partners, Bristol
MAIN CONTRACTOR
Sir Robert McAlpine Ltd

Some Bristolians had come to regard office blocks as a ritual hate object. One Bridewell Street, developed by MEPC to be the regional office of accountants Ernst & Young, demonstrated that an office block (or at least a bespoke office block) can be elegant, civilised and witty - can, indeed, reinvigorate a drab and dejected townscape. Because of traffic noise and pollution, the building looks inwards on to a full-height, naturally-lit atrium. Its protective exterior is clad in white panels with cheerful, well-detailed red trimming. Offices can be good for the city centre scene.

53 Renewal and Conservation: a. Centre Gate House; b. St Bartholemew's Hospital; c. St Bartholemew's; d. Christmas Steps and Colston Street, 1982-1990 Moxley Jenner & Partners, Alec French Partnership, Peter Ware, Richard Pedlar

The spate of 1960s and '70s office- and road-building blighted and scarred a whole section of central Bristol between The Centre and Broadmead. The well-loved view down historic Christmas Steps, for instance, was left open and naked to roaring traffic. Moxley Jenner & Partners designed the office development Centre Gate with the lower 4-storey block to the right to close the vista and restore tranquillity to this oasis of antiquity. The pedestrian route runs behind and partly in colonnade; servicing is from the rear.

Just to the north at St Bartholemew's Hospital the same practice gave fresh life to this remains of a monastic enclave by restoration of buildings from medieval to 19th century (including Bristol's first purpose-built flats) and sympathetic but functional infill. Alec French Partnership fitted the money-spinning office scheme St Bartholemew's round this with ingenuity and tact.

Christmas Steps itself and the ancient, typically timber-framed buildings at its top and bottom are deep in the psyche of Bristolians, a historic enclave regarded with pride by citizens and council alike. Yet by the 1980s all was not well; many of the buildings were deteriorating and empty or underused. Again a co-ordinated approach was needed, but nothing happened. It took an architect, Peter Ware, looking wider than a single plot or single client, to push things forward. He went before a sceptical council committee and talked with such conviction and authority about the need for comprehensive refurbishment and how it could be done that he won them over.

The city pushed the scheme forward, and Peter had the satisfaction of carrying out the exemplary restoration of the crucial gateway group of buildings at the head of the Steps in Colston Street. Working closely with him, Richard Pedlar was responsible for restoring and adapting No 15 Christmas Steps - a building part medieval, part 18th- and part 19th-century - to provide an art gallery with workshop and living accommodation above.

↖ **Centre Gate House** (53a)
City Centre, Bristol, BS1
CLIENT
Centros Properties, Bristol Municipal Charities
ARCHITECT
Moxley Jenner & Partners
QUANTITY SURVEYOR
Centros Properties in-house
STRUCTURAL ENGINEER
Roughton & Fenton
MAIN CONTRACTOR
Cowlin

← **St Bartholomew's Hospital** (53b)
City Centre, Bristol, BS1
CLIENT
Bristol Municipal Charities
ARCHITECT
Moxley Jenner & Partners
QUANTITY SURVEYOR
Moxley Jenner & Partners
STRUCTURAL ENGINEER
Roughton & Fenton
LANDSCAPE ARCHITECT
Moxley Jenner & Partners
MAIN CONTRACTOR
C H Pearce

St Bartholomew's *(53c)*
(not shown)
City Centre, Bristol, BS1
CLIENT
Haslemere Estates
ARCHITECT
Alec French Partnership
QUANTITY SURVEYOR
Gleeds

STRUCTURAL ENGINEER
Ove Arup Partnership
MECHANICAL AND
ELECTRICAL CONSULTANT
Hoare Lea Partnership
ARTIST
David Backhouse
MAIN CONTRACTOR
C H Pearce Construction

↑ **Christmas Steps/
Colston Street** *(53d)*
City Centre, Bristol, BS1
CLIENT
Bristol City Council and
individual owners
ARCHITECTS
Peter Ware; Richard
Pedlar Chartered
Architects

**St Augustine's Court
- south building** (54a)
(not shown)
City Centre, Bristol, BS1
ARCHITECT
Moxley Jenner &
Partners

↑ **St Augustine's
Court - main
development** (54b)
City Centre, Bristol, BS1
CLIENT AND PRESENT
OWNER
Legal & General
Assurance Society Ltd
ARCHITECT
Stride Treglown Ltd

QUANTITY SURVEYOR
Gleeds
STRUCTURAL ENGINEER
Clarke Bond Partnership
MECHANICAL AND
ELECTRICAL ENGINEER
Fergusons
MAIN CONTRACTOR
Laing Management

**No 31 Great George →
Street** (55)
Bristol, BS1
CLIENT
The Church
Commissioners for
England
ARCHITECT
Alec French Partnership,
Bristol
QUANTITY SURVEYOR
Gordon Harris & Partners,
Bristol
STRUCTURAL ENGINEER
T M Ventham, Bristol
MECHANICAL AND
ELECTRICAL CONSULTANT
Hoare Lea, Bristol
MAIN CONTRACTOR
Laing South-West

54 St Augustine's Parade, St Augustine's Court, c.1988-1990
Moxley Jenner & Partners, Stride Treglown

Some 400m away to the south of the Christmas Steps scheme stands another familiar part of the Bristol townscape, St Augustine's Parade. Behind its varied frontages lay a maze of decaying yards and buildings. Moxley Jenner & Partners demonstrated how these could be brought to life again (here, too, the keys were access and co-operation by landowners); they then restored and converted one old warehouse to office use. Stride Treglown carried out a second, more extensive scheme with a second warehouse and taller, brick-clad buildings round a service court.

55 No 31 Great George Street, 1987
Alec French Partnership

The site of this building - a prominent hillside adjoining the parkland of Brandon Hill, and in a conservation area - was previously occupied by an ugly, obtrusive office block. The architects' achievement was to devise a sympathetic but commercially viable replacement, thus making it possible to demolish the eyesore. The new building's Great George Street elevation consists of two pavilions framing the entrance bay and is in scale and harmony with adjacent Georgian terraces. Behind this it steps down the hillside with terraces, planting, and a curved bay facing Brandon Hill. A thoroughly functional building, it nonetheless has a romantic picturesqueness which sits well in this parkland setting.

↖ **Spectrum** *(56)*
Bond Street, Bristol, BS1
CLIENT
Prudential
ARCHITECT
BGP Group Architects,
Bristol
QUANTITY SURVEYOR
Banks Wood & Partners
CONSULTANT ENGINEER
Keith Parsons
Partnership
MAIN CONTRACTOR
Espley-Tyas Construction

56 Spectrum, 1984
BGP Group Architects

Spectrum is a gateway building, alongside what is effectively the terminus of the M32 motorway. Clad in glass and air-conditioned to insulate it from traffic noise and fumes, it was at first much criticised by Bristolians. Now they are used to it, they recognise it as one of the city's most striking buildings, and some of them have grown quite fond of it. Another building right for its particular setting.

57 BBC Regional Headquarters, 1987
BBC Architects

This is not by any stretch of imagination the best post-war building in Clifton, but to judge it fairly you need to know how it came about, what the site was like beforehand, and what might have gone there if the client had had its way. In the 1980s the BBC was intent on building a series of network production centres containing large amounts of studio space heavily serviced with what were then regarded as essential cabling and ductwork. Its existing complex included one of the original Whiteladies Road Italianate villas, one later gothic revival house, an unsightly surface car park, and a large shed-like building containing studio space.

The BBC wished, not unreasonably, to put its network centre into a single building, and ran what was virtually an internal design competition for its in-house architects to come up with a scheme. At various times its architects produced at least four different schemes; its strong-willed chairman at that time, George Howard (of Castle Howard), threw his considerable weight into the fray; and the scheme that nearly got built would have clad the Whiteladies as well as the Belgrave Road frontage in glass curtain-walling.

The city planners pointed out that this was unlikely to fulfil the requirement that a building should "conserve or enhance" the character of the conservation area; and eventually - with considerable help from an architect in the planning department - they came up with this Bath stone-clad pastiche: two respectably Italianate pavilions joined to each other and to the existing villa by recessed link-blocks.

BBC Regional Headquarters (57)
Whiteladies Road, Clifton
CLIENT
BBC
ARCHITECT
BBC Architects
quantity surveyor:
Gleeds
STRUCTURAL ENGINEER
BBC
MECHANICAL AND
ELECTRICAL CONSULTANT
Hoare Lea & Partners
LANDSCAPE ARCHITECT
BBC
MAIN CONTRACTOR
R M Douglas

The scheme sacrificed the gothic curiosity, but it got rid of the shed and surface car park. The columned main entrance (the left-hand link-block) looks too squashed for its purpose; the roofs are distinctly awkward and have not weathered as must have been hoped; and turning the corner into Belgrave Road to find three-storey-high glass walls is disconcerting. The big gain, however, which justifies all the unsatisfactory compromise, is that this stretch of Whiteladies Road remains sandstone and Italianate; both the overall style and the rhythm of the townscape are preserved.

The BBC, incidentally, no longer needs nor wants grand, purpose-built network production centres. New technology and contracted-out production have made them redundant; flexible office-style buildings are the order of the day. The Whiteladies Road buildings are now - as probably most outsiders thought they always were - the corporation's regional headquarters.

58 University of Bristol Arts Faculty, 1985
MacCormac Jamieson Prichard

A skilful piece of infill and regeneration in a conservation area, this Arts Faculty development consists of refurbished Victorian villas and new, single-storey teaching buildings in their back gardens. Each new block is L-shaped, linking to the corresponding villa and opening on to a south-facing courtyard garden. The development had to meet stringent conservation area constraints and tight University Grants Committee cost limits. It may have benefited: in line and materials the additions show an almost oriental lightness of touch. A high-level walkway provides a new pedestrian spine and unobtrusive means of escape from the houses.

← **Arts Faculty, Woodland Road** (58)
Woodland Road, Bristol BS8
CLIENT AND OWNER
University of Bristol
ARCHITECT
MacCormac Jamieson Prichard
STRUCTURAL ENGINEER
Ove Arup & Partners
QUANTITY SURVEYOR
Hamilton H Turner & Son
MECHANICAL AND ELECTRICAL CONSULTANT
Ove Arup & Partners
MAIN CONTRACTOR
Ernest Ireland Construction Ltd, Bristol

Carfax Court (59) →
Durdham Down,
Westbury Park, BS9
CLIENT
Retirement Properties Ltd
OWNER
individual owner-
occupiers
ARCHITECT
Ferguson Mann Architects
QUANTITY SURVEYOR
Gleeds
STRUCTURAL ENGINEER
Ken Brown
LANDSCAPE ARCHITECT
Balston & Co
MAIN CONTRACTOR
Sir Robert MacAlpine

59 Carfax Court, 1989
Ferguson Mann Architects

Carfax Court stands on the edge of the Durdham Down parkland,
abutting a spacious Victorian and Edwardian suburb. This development of owner-occupier retirement flats is arranged round a
"collegiate" courtyard and incorporates two large Victorian
houses. The layout, together with lower parking standards for
sheltered housing, enabled Ferguson Mann to provide 20 spacious
new two-bedroom flats; the houses yielded eight more plus
communal facilities. The arch under the clocktower offers an
alluring vista to the Downs beyond. Stylistic elements include
strong mullions. If this is pastiche, then long live good pastiche!

60 Watershed (re-use of transit sheds), 1982
J T Design Build, Bush Consultancy

The line of buildings running from the Centre along the west side of St Augustine's Reach and now known as Watershed are sometimes described as dock warehouses. They were in fact built in the 1890s as transit sheds - the temporary, covered resting and marshalling place for goods unloaded from ships and awaiting shipment by rail, or vice versa. In the absence of the railway

sidings which used to cover much of Canon's Marsh, we tend to overlook this.

The Port of Bristol's move downriver made such buildings redundant, and in the 1980s the port authority granted a long lease of the two sheds nearest the Centre to the JT Group. JT refurbished and adapted them to accommodate an arts centre, a local radio station (the present GWR) and leisure uses such as bars, cafés and shops. It was a forward-looking plan which, as with many pioneering ventures, was slow to take off commercially. In recent years Watershed has become increasingly popular, and Pero's Bridge has brought a new and gratifyingly heavy "footfall" to the building.

The bridge, indeed, made the replacement of a third shed, "U", which was seriously affected by concrete decay, a commercial proposition. JT completed it in 1998, and at the time of writing were planning to refurbish and convert a transit shed downstream of the bridge, "V". Though these were essentially very functional buildings, their waterside elevations have a rhythm and poetry to them; and the Port Authority could not resist turning the gable end of "E" shed, facing on to the centre, into something of a showpiece.

61 Stonewest House, 1983
Ferguson Mann Architects

The site, in leafy Victorian Clifton, was a mish-mash of wooden garages and unsightly decay. It adjoined a rather grand three-storey Georgian detached house fronting on to Oakfield Road, whose owner wanted to move into a new office block. This the architects provided in a largely two-storey range linked to an existing lodge by a recessed single-storey extension. Walls are pennant stone at base, above that rendered blockwork; roofs are slate, and the two-storey block is topped by a functional but rather jolly lantern, bringing natural light to the spaces below.

Visually it all works so well that, at a very casual glance, you might take it for a recently refurbished bit of the Victorian townscape. Any more than a casual glance tells you it is a no-pretences 1980s building, but with scale, fenestration and materials so well chosen that it fits beautifully into the conservation area, yet has its own quiet but strong personality. When well done, as here, this kind of conservation area architecture looks effortless: in fact it requires a great deal of hard work to get it right, as well as sensitivity and originality of design.

Fitting honest new buildings into conservation areas is an art to which most architects pay lip service, but fewer have mastered. The late Sir Basil Spence once explained it to me thus: "It is," he said, "a matter of designing buildings of the right blood group". An apt metaphor - but he didn't by any means always get it right either.

↑ **Stonewest House** (61)
Oakfield Grove,
Clifton, BS8
CLIENT
Stonewest Ltd
ARCHITECT
Ferguson Mann Architects
STRUCTURAL ENGINEER
Mander, Raikes & Marshall
MECHANICAL AND
ELECTRICAL CONSULTANT
Coordinated Design
Practice
MAIN CONTRACTOR
R L Wright
(Contractors) Ltd

← **Watershed, E Shed** (60)
St Augustine's Reach, BS1
CLIENT
JT Developments
ARCHITECT
JT Design Build Watershed,
W Shed
CLIENT
JT Developments
ARCHITECT
Bush Consultancy

62 Garden Court, 1983
Vic Love of Hubbard Ford Partnership

The brief was to convert the former church hall of All Saints into as many single-bedroom flats as possible. To maximise natural light the architect decided to demolish a large entrance wing, preserving the facing stones for re-use. The division of the main hall's volume was ingenious, retaining as much of the external walls as possible; combining recycled stone with reconstituted stone cast on site from Bath stone dust; pushing out balconies at first-floor and roof levels; and shaping new window and door openings to emphasise the original gothic character of the building.

The scheme yielded 12 one-bedroom flats and one maisonette, plus a public garden at the front and walled private gardens at the rear. All flats were sold by completion and continue to be popular. Vic Love's alterations to the original structure look as if they had always been there; yet this is not tame pastiche - it has its own strong, likeable personality, and was a gain to the streetscape. It had a delicious spire, which came down in the 1987 gales. Rumour has it that this is in store somewhere. If so, the owners should put it up again.

← **Garden Court** (62)
Alma Vale Road,
Clifton, BS8
CLIENT
Steadman Fox
PRESENT OWNER
Magician Ltd
ARCHITECT
Vic Love (project architect), Hubbard Ford Partnership
QUANTITY SURVEYOR
Hubbard Ford Partnership
STRUCTURAL ENGINEER
Crier Liddiard
MAIN CONTRACTOR
Robert Cox Construction

↓ **Brick Sculpture, Bristol Eye Hospital** (63)
Lower Maudlin Street, City Centre, BS1
CLIENT
Bristol & Weston Health Authority
SCULPTOR
Walter Ritchie

63 Brick Sculpture, Bristol Eye Hospital, 1986
Walter Ritchie

Most people approve of public art in principle, but they often dislike particular examples in practice. This brick bas-relief, actually sculpted into the facing brick of the Eye Hospital, is deservedly popular (even if the building isn't) because its subject is directly connected with what goes on inside. There is a respectable argument against public art which is "applied to" buildings, rather than forming part of their design and public spaces: the "lipstick on the gorilla" syndrome. Such works all too often have only a tenuous connection with the buildings, and look like (indeed, often are) an afterthought. That criticism does not apply here. The sculpture is relevant and, in addition to its intrinsic quality as art, it improves an adjacent public space - even though that public space is only the pavement of Lower Maudlin Street.

7

Changing gear
1990-99

The 1990s were a time of great change, with the need to renew Bristol's urban fabric often seemingly at war with out-of-town development in Bristol's northern fringe; and a growing public interest in urban design and "green" buildings not always matched by developers' narrow commercial objectives.

**Lloyds Bank
Headquarters** *(64)*
Canon's Marsh, BS1
CLIENT
Lloyds Project
Construction Co Ltd for
Lloyds Bank plc
PRESENT OWNER
Lloyds TSB plc
ARCHITECT
Arup Associates
QUANTITY SURVEYOR
Arup Associates
ENGINEERING CONSUL-
TANTS
Arup Associates
LANDSCAPE ARCHITECT
Peter Swann Associates
MAIN CONTRACTOR
Bovis Construction Ltd

64 Lloyds Bank Headquarters, 1992
Arup Associates

Canon's Marsh, an area of redundant industrial land between the cathedral and the old commercial waterside, had stubbornly resisted attempts at urban renewal: though it was close to the city centre, it was perceived as inaccessible and desolate. Lloyds Bank, needing a new high-tech headquarters building, had the far-sightedness to see the site's potential - and engaged respected national architects Arup Associates to design it.

The Stage 1 building - a columned crescent facing the

Floating Harbour across a new public piazza - has a presence and authority which supplied the catalyst to the whole area's current regeneration. Stage 2, just to the west, is a circular "doughnut" building. Both seem to strive after a modern reworking of classicism - but not totally successfully. A more serious criticism is that they are not appropriate to the location. These are campus buildings set down in an area that called for dense, fine-grained development. They waste waterside space that may soon be at a premium. But they did kickstart the Canon's Marsh revival.

RAC Supercentre *(65)*
Great Park Road,
Almondsbury, BS32,
CLIENT AND OWNER
RAC Motoring Services
ARCHITECT
Nicholas Grimshaw &
Partners
QUANTITY SURVEYOR
Hanscomb
STRUCTURAL ENGINEER
Alan Baxter Associates
**ENVIRONMENTAL
ENGINEER**
Ove Arup & Partners
LANDSCAPE ARCHITECT
Edwards Gale
**MANAGEMENT
CONTRACTOR**
Bovis Contractors
STEELWORK
R Glazzard
GLAZING
Permasteelisa (UK)

65 RAC Bradley Stoke Supercentre, 1994
Nicholas Grimshaw & Partners

If we have to have a celebration of the motorway age, the M4/M5 junction is the place for it, and this building is a splendid celebration. It signals its presence by two tall masts above a cylindrical stair-tower from which projects the Crow's Nest, a high-level meeting room with views over the Bristol Channel and

Bristol's fast-developing northern fringe.

Below is the actual building - in plan, like the crow's nest, a curved triangle, but much bigger. From a ground-floor base with concrete columns, the dark glass walls of first and second floors curve upwards and outwards, broken horizontally by a fringe of brises-soleil. Inside, open-plan work areas designed for hot-desking, look into a triangular atrium in which hangs a complex three-directional, open staircase. The blue steel columns of a lift-shaft assist orientation. The second floor, which stops short of the exterior glazing, has a sail-like roof; throughout, rails, stairs, and even exposed, exaggerated ventilation ducts create the illusion that we are on an ocean-going liner. Terrific PR for the RAC, and - as control and call centres go - an agreeable place to work.

↑ **College Green** (66)
Bristol, BS1

PARTNERS
Bristol City Council, Bristol
Cathedral, Vaux Group
(Swallow Royal Hotels),
English Partnerships

DESIGNER
Bristol City Council, City
Centre Projects & Urban
Design Team

CIVIL ENGINEER
Bristol City Council,
Engineering Design Team

LANDSCAPE
Bristol City Council,
Natural Environment
Team

CONTRACTORS
SITA Contract Services,
Bristol; P Trant Ltd,
Gloucester; Costain
Construction, Cardiff

66 College Green refurbishment, 1991
Bristol City Council

For several decades what should have been an attractive pedestrian space and tranquil setting for the cathedral was ruined by heavy traffic. Then the city boldly closed the road in front of the cathedral, and in 1991 transformed it by a skilful combination of hard and soft landscape. College Green is now an enjoyable public place, popular with both citizens and visitors. Unexpectedly it has a new visual focus: the eye is drawn once more towards the cathedral.

67 Bristol Crown Court, 1994
Stride Treglown

The Lord Chancellor's Department, when it first proposed replacing the city's law courts, seemed determined to move them out of the historic centre. This, argued opponents, would be bad both for court efficiency and the area's vitality. The Department relented, agreeing to build behind the retained Victorian and Edwardian facades of Bristol's former main post office. Architects Stride Treglown contrived to fit a completely new 10-court complex into the site, but this required pushing the building up above existing rooftops. This is well managed: the new roofline as seen from The Centre is dramatic, and reminds us that the historic centre stands on a hill.

Crown Court (67) ↗
Small Street, BS1
CLIENT AND OWNER →
Court Service, Lord Chancellor's Department
ARCHITECT
Stride Treglown
STRUCTURAL ENGINEER
Clarke Bond Partnership
MECHANICAL AND ELECTRICAL ENGINEER
Fergusons
QUANTITY SURVEYOR
Symonds
LANDSCAPE ARCHITECT
PSA
MAIN CONTRACTOR
Taylor Woodrow (Southern) Ltd

68 Ministry of Defence Procurement Executive, 1996
Percy Thomas Partnership

The MOD's Procurement Executive, which buys £5.5-billion of equipment a year and has 4,400 staff, was previously housed in 15 separate offices. This new complex, in Bristol's northern fringe, brings them all together and - given its out-of-town location - makes a fair fist of doing so in an environmentally friendly fashion. The complex is, for instance, CFC-free; is low energy, with optimum orientation and insulation and use of displacement ventilation, not air-conditioning; and, thanks to the 5,000 trees and 28,000 shrubs planted, it is neutral on carbon dioxide emissions. It even has its own railway station.

Abbey Wood is more like a small town than a building: it consists of four office "neighbourhoods", a circular business library and a nursery for 100 babies and toddlers. Each neighbourhood centres on a linear atrium or "glazed street", and this and the materials used make for a pleasantly light and open ambience. The landscape, with its 5-acre lake and cascade, was central to the planning, as was quality. In contrast to so many public sector projects, the client was ready to spend more on quality in order to produce an excellent working environment and save money later.

**MOD Abbey
Wood** (68)
Abbey Wood,
Stoke Gifford, BS34
CLIENT AND OWNER
MOD Procurement
Executive
ARCHITECT
Percy Thomas
Partnership
(Architects) Ltd
QUANTITY SURVEYOR
Bucknall Austin
STRUCTURAL ENGINEER
Ernest Green Partnership
SERVICES ENGINEER
Hoare Lee & Partners
LANDSCAPE ARCHITECT
PTP Landscape
PROJECT MANAGER
Symonds Project
Managers
MAIN CONTRACTOR
(SHELL AND CORE)
John Mowlem
CONSTRUCTION (FIT-OUT)
Symonds Woolf
Aztec West

69 Aztec West, 1981 onwards
John Outram Associates, Thorpe Architecture and others

In its early days Aztec West won much attention from architectural commentators both for a master plan drawn up by Nicholas Grimshaw & Partners and for its policy of commissioning nationally and internationally known architects for individual buildings. Under its original developers, the electricity industry pension fund ESN, this seems to have taken the form of "token hunting" - you had to have a Grimshaw building, an Outram, a CZGW. At least one well-known architect was told, "We've seen your building at x; could you do us one just like it, please?" This, of course, is not the way to get the best out of an architect, and though the building was completed and apparently regarded by the client as satisfactory, the architect was left feeling very unsatisfied with the whole process.

The present owners Arlington rely for their master-planning on the Arundel practice Thorpe Architecture, who have also designed a number of the individual buildings. Some of the buildings we would have liked to feature we were, for "security" reasons, not permitted to photograph. The whole of Aztec West, though it looks like public realm, is private property, strictly controlled by security staff, and members of the public have no automatic right to be there or take pictures. It is a strange reflection on late 20th century society that it was easier to take the photos we wanted at the Ministry of Defence's establishment charged with the procurement of weapons than at a high profile business park.

Whatever one thinks of individual buildings at Aztec West, the landscape setting is of an undoubted high quality. Various landscape designers have had a hand in it, including Clouston (our picture) and Thorpe Architecture. The same profound objections apply to this as to the Cribbs Causeway shopping mall and other "northern fringe" developments: they almost demand that those who work or visit arrive by car. They therefore generate car

↑ **Units 1200-1220** (69a)
Park Avenue,
Almondsbury, BS
CLIENT
Electricity Supply
Nominees
ARCHITECT
John Outram Associates
QUANTITY SURVEYOR
Bucknall Austin
Partnership
STRUCTURAL ENGINEER
Tony Godfrey
LANDSCAPE ARCHITECT
Robert Holden
MAIN CONTRACTOR
Beazers

Aztec Centre (69b) →
Park Avenue,
Almondsbury, BS
CLIENT
Arlington plc
ARCHITECT
Thorpe Architecture
QUANTITY SURVEYOR
Gleeds
STRUCTURAL ENGINEER
Peter Brett Associates
MECHANICAL AND
ELECTRICAL ENGINEER
Ferguson & Partners
LANDSCAPE ARCHITECT
PTP Landscape
MAIN CONTRACTOR
Sir Robert McAlpine

Lake and surrounding →
landscape (69c)
Park Avenue,
Almondsbury, BS
CLIENT
ESN
LANDSCAPE ARCHITECT
Brian Clouston & Partners

traffic which, at peak, the road network cannot cope with, and encourage people to use cars, not public transport.

Units 1200-1220 are distinctively Outram, with his chunky use of brick, feeling for colour and nice detail. Unlike some of its neighbours, this is not an "anywhere building": it seems to say "This place houses industry, not offices" - which is true, but odd in terms of traditional business park mix. Perhaps not John Outram's best, but one of Aztec's undoubted successes. The Aztec Centre, which is the place from which Aztec West is managed, is externally an unrevealing glass box. Its best feature is the very generous, and generously landscaped, atrium, which then leads on into an external landscape centring on a formal tree-lined walk.

70 The Mall, 1998
Building Design Partnership

The good things about the Cribbs Causeway shopping centre are a key location on the national motorway network within easy driving distance of a million or so people and parking for 7,000 cars; the bad things are likewise its key location on the national motorway network within easy driving distance of a million of so people and parking for 7,000 cars. It should never have been permitted. It is a huge generator of car journeys, and although it has its own so-called bus station (a collection of bus stands, bus stops and bus shelters), the journey from most places in Bristol is so slow that no-one with use of a car is likely to forego its use. Even if Cribbs Causeway had, like Sheffield's Meadowhall, a rapid transit link to the city, these formidable objections would remain.

That said, the architects, given their brief, have done well. They explain that such super-centres have a standard dumbbell shape, with the anchor stores (here M&S and John Lewis) at either end. On a first visit to Cribbs, I found it bore a resemblance to the French Eurocité near Calais - but it is much better. The dumbbell is hinged in the middle, with a third leg containing a food court joining it at this central point. It makes skilful use of the fall of the land to provide "ground floor" access at both its two levels; the architects have also avoided the claustrophobic effect that closed-in malls too often have by providing huge "windows" out into the south Gloucestershire landscape, typically wherever you sit down to eat or drink.

The building, both inside and out, avoids rhetoric and - unlike too many malls - eschews tacked-on decoration. Care has been taken to ensure clear sightlines and to make the layout readily comprehensible to strangers. It does quite well on energy conservation: it has a glass roof with daytime solar shading and a degree of reflectivity to avoid a night-time "black hole" effect. Its heating and ventilation system is, as one would now expect, low velocity, with gentle air currents. But what a contradiction to have a building which saves energy while filling those 7,000 car spaces with mostly undesirable and unnecessary journeys. I repeat: it should never have been permitted.

The Mall, Cribbs Causeway (70)
Cribbs Causeway, BS34
CLIENT
Prudential and J T Baylis, joint developers
ARCHITECT
Building Design Partnership
QUANTITY SURVEYOR
Gardiner & Theobald
STRUCTURAL ENGINEER
Ove Arup & Partners
MECHANICAL AND ELECTRICAL CONSULTANTS
Hoare Lea & Partners
TRAFFIC CONSULTANTS
Symonds
PROJECT MANAGER
Heery International
LANDSCAPE ARCHITECT
Building Design Partnership
MAIN CONTRACTOR
Bovis Construction

71 St James's Court, 1996
Holder Mathias Alcock

The St James's Parade conservation area has been described as "an oasis of tranquillity in a harsh urban environment". A well-treed little park screens the terrace from traffic; two stone towers stand guard: St James's Church, survival of a 12th-century priory, and that of a 19th-century chapel. In between, HMA demolished a dull 1950s office block and built this attractive new building. In Bath stone and biscuit-coloured brick, it reinforces the line of the former terrace; fits in 3,500 sq metres of floorspace in just three storeys. Elegant use of square window bays and sun-deflecting louvres. A good fit.

72 Merchant Venturers Building/University Gate, 1996
Atkins Walters Webster Architects

Merchant Venturers/University Gate expresses graphically the new entrepreneurialism of British universities. On a steep hillside, it has an uphill entrance, to Engineering Faculty lecture rooms and offices; and a downhill entrance, on Park Row, to the commercial office space of University Gate. At its heart a tall thin atrium provides a pleasant social space. The building does no visual violence to the adjacent Wills Building and has an attractive roofline, but some of its stylistic juxtapositions - notably on the Park Row elevation - are less than happy.

← **St James's Court** (71)
St James's Parade, BS1
CLIENT
Scottish Mutual
Assurance plc
PROJECT MANAGER
Osprey Project
Management
ARCHITECT
Holder Mathias Alcock
plc
QUANTITY SURVEYOR
Franklin & Andrews
STRUCTURAL AND CIVIL
ENGINEER
Clarke Bond Partnership
MAIN CONTRACTOR
Higgs & Hill Western Ltd

University Gate (72) →
Park Row, Clifton, BS8
CLIENT AND OWNER
University of Bristol
ARCHITECT
Atkins Walters Webster
Architects
STRUCTURAL ENGINEER
Ove Arup & Partners
(Bristol)
QUANTITY SURVEYOR
Bucknall Austin plc
MECHANICAL AND
ELECTRICAL CONSULTANT
Hoare Lea & Partners
LANDSCAPE CONSULTANT
University of Bristol
Gardens Department
MAIN CONTRACTOR
Pearce Construction

73 WCA Warehouse conversion, 1997
Architecton

Built around 1910 as prestige offices and warehousing for the Western Counties Agricultural Co-operative, the WCA building is one of Bristol's earliest concrete-framed buildings. It stood empty for many years and damp penetrated the structure causing decay. In 1986 the city council as freeholder mounted a competition for schemes to convert it into housing, which Architecton won; but the developer withdrew and the building stood empty for another decade, until Bristol Churches Housing Association raised funding for an amended scheme.

The WCA building now provides 39 flats instead of the 28 originally proposed. It does so without seriously affecting the appearance of this listed building, using two main devices. First, by carefully phased demolition the architects carved out a courtyard at third floor level, through which rises a central, structurally independent lift-and-stair tower. Secondly it provides four flats in two penthouses - a straightforward modern addition but relatively unobtrusive.

Both flats and common spaces have a distinctive character, which Architecton's conversion has reinforced. Some waterside flats, for instance, have quirky little extra rooms created from the hoist canopies. Means of escape in case of fire is provided by segregating a thin slice of the building inside its end walls which contains stairs leading to separate exit doors.

WCA is important both as a pioneer of construction methods and as a key piece of townscape. It has at last been saved, and contributes usefully to bringing people back to live in the centre of the city. It also provides - as a piece of "planning gain" - one more link in the waterside promenade which, with development or conversion on adjoining sites, should soon be complete from Bristol Bridge to Redcliffe Bridge.

WCA Warehouse conversion *(73)*
Redcliffe Backs, Bristol, BS1
CLIENT
Bristol Churches Housing Association
PRESENT OWNER
Bristol Churches Housing Association

ARCHITECT
Architecton
QUANTITY SURVEYOR
Colin Jenkins Partnership
STRUCTURAL ENGINEER
Hyder Consulting
MAIN CONTRACTOR
Russell Construction, Clevedon

Redcliffe Quay *(74)*
Redcliff Street, Bristol 1
CLIENT
Standard Life
Assurance Co
ARCHITECT
Alec French Partnership
QUANTITY SURVEYOR
Gleeds, Bristol
STRUCTURAL ENGINEER
Ove Arup & Partners,
Bristol
MECHANICAL AND
ELECTRICAL CONSULTANT
Hoare Lea & Partners,
Bristol
PROJECT MANAGER
Laing Construction
Management

74 Redcliffe Quay, 1991
Alec French Partnership

Part of that continuous riverside walk is provided by Redcliffe Quay. This is a large infill office development which, while unashamedly modern, contrives to harmonise with the character of this part of the Floating Harbour, a conservation area histori-cally dominated by tall brick warehouses, many of them lost in World War II. The scheme consists of two buildings separated by a piazza. The southern building - a series of linked six-storey pavilions - is several times larger than its northern neighbour. This is a reflection of the city planners' wish to open up a vista from King Street on the other side of the water to the tower of St Thomas's church.

The piazza, whose centrepiece is a sculpture evoking the spirit of exploration, also provides a link from the waterside promenade into the hinterland. The main building is arranged round an atrium with lifts, stairs, and galleries for horizontal movement: it is thus a natural, lively meeting place. The long waterside frontage of the south building is broken up by recesses between its three large pavilions. Light buff facing materials - stone and brick - and balconies give a lighter feel to what could easily have been an over-dominant building. Ground-level café use with tables by the waterside helps to ensure that Redcliffe Quay plays a positive role in the opening up of the waterside.

River Station *(75)*
The Grove,
City Centre, BS1
CLIENT
Riverstation Partnership
ARCHITECT
Inscape Architects
STRUCTURAL ENGINEER
Christopher Fitton
Associates
MECHANICAL CONSULTANT
Building Services Solutions
ELECTRICAL CONSULTANT
Severn Control
Systems Ltd
MAIN CONTRACTOR
Inscape Project
Management Ltd

75 River Station, 1998
Inscape Architects

What looks like a completely new waterside building of very
nautical character is in fact the conversion of a former river
police station - hence the name. It involved flooring over an
internal slipway and dock to create extra floor space, and
extending the building at first floor level over what was a flat
roof. Works were designed to ensure minimum interference with
the listed quay. All this has been done with a sureness of touch
which makes the result seem inevitable - especially the waterside
elevation with its large windows and balconies with canvas
awnings looking out over the water, and a roofline evocative,
according to your bent, of shells, waves or sails - but instantly
identified with water and ships.

Internally the impression is of cleanness of line and a limited
palette of high quality materials. Many of these benefited from a
"pulled-up-by-its-bootstraps" element of the scheme. After
carrying out its feasibility study, Inscape put in a planning appli-
cation and this generated commercial interest in the site and its
surroundings, so that the client felt able to spend more on the
building. The upgrade covered both materials and performance:
better thermal and acoustic performance, for instance. Unlike
many bars and restaurants these days, River Station does not have
noise bouncing back and forth from surfaces and furniture. It is a
delightful place to eat in, and a delight to look at from the water
or from the Redcliffe bank. Creative re-use at its best.

76 Poole's Wharf, 1999
Philip Thorpe

Architects tend to be sniffy about buildings designed by a developer's in-house staff, and suspicious (often justifiably) about anyone calling himself "architectural design consultant". It usually means they haven't passed all the exams. But by their fruits ye shall know them ... and the fruits in this case are by no means bad.

The site was, of course, a peach, but the development not only exploits views out across the water, but takes some trouble in its arrangements of heights and skylines to protect views of Hotwells and Clifton. It also seeks, with fair success, to catch the spirit of Regency houses up the hill. At its heart is a nice little garden square; and the public waterside walk and linking footbridge (no doubt required by the planners) are well and ungrudgingly done.

This is not brilliant architecture, but it is an advance on earlier residential development across the water at Baltic Wharf. It does not pretend to be Georgian or Regency and, while some of the details are a shade awkward, it adds up to a real place with a personality of its own. Others working on the Bristol waterside will no doubt strive to better it, and all strength to their arms.

Poole's Wharf *(76)*
Poole's Wharf Court,
Rownham Mead, BS8
CLIENT
Crest Homes
(South West) Ltd
ARCHITECT
Philip Thorpe
(Crest in-house architect)
DETAILED DESIGN
BBA, Bath
QUANTITY SURVEYOR
Crest Homes
STRUCTURAL ENGINEER
Symonds Travers Morgan
MECHANICAL AND
ELECTRICAL
Symonds Travers Morgan
and in-house
LANDSCAPE ARCHITECT
Symonds Travers Morgan
BRIDGE DESIGN
HLD Ltd
CONTRACT MANGEMENT
Crest Homes
(South West) Ltd

77 Marketing & Exhibition Centre, 1992
Alec French Partnership

Bristol Development Corporation wanted an exhibition building to display its proposals for regenerating the city's east-central area. It needed to fit a cleared waterside, but had to be moveable. AFP's design marries functional requirements with a strikingly maritime appearance. The drum-shaped exhibition area is surmounted by viewing platform sheltered by sail-like canopy, with a crow's nest for more distant views, and the CCTV equivalent of a camera obscura. The central mast is key to its demountability.

Marketing & →
Exhibition Centre *(77)*
Avon Street, BS2
CLIENT
Bristol Development
Corporation
PRESENT OWNER
English Partnerships
ARCHITECT
Alec French Partnership
ENGINEERING CONSULTANT
Whitby & Bird, Bath
QUANTITY SURVEYOR
James Nisbet &
Partners, Bath
EXHIBITION DESIGN
Proctor & Stevenson,
Bristol
MAIN CONTRACTOR
Pearce Construction

↑ **The Architecture** →
Centre *(78)*
Narrow Quay, BS1

CLIENT AND OWNER
Bristol Centre for the
Advancement of
Architecture
ARCHITECT
Niall Phillips Architects Ltd
QUANTITY SURVEYOR
Gardiner & Theobald
STRUCTURAL ENGINEER
Hyder Consultancy
MECHANICAL AND
ELECTRICAL CONSULTANT
Ove Arup & Partners
MAIN CONTRACTOR
Property Enhancement
(Bristol) Ltd

78 The Architecture Centre, 1996
Niall Phillips Architects

Bristol's Architecture Centre serves both as showcase for architects' work and focus for involving a wider public in architecture. Significantly it is not a new building but a skilful low-budget reuse of an old one: a burnt-out, rubble-walled four-storey warehouse on the waterside in the heart of a regenerated arts and entertainment area. A concrete ring-beam supports the roof; lifts, service core and stairs have been fitted in with minimum interference; and many features of the 200-year-old building repaired and retained. The showcase is itself a showcase.

79 Ecohouse, 1997
Exedra D S Drage

This house, and the Ecohome below, both have a "green" objective, but go about achieving it in different ways. The Redland Ecohouse was a speculative venture by an enlightened developer, subsequently bought and now lived in by an enlightened owner-occupier. It uses "brown land" (the site of an electricity sub-station); its materials include reused stone; and it eschews all but the most basic technology - no solar panels, but optimum orientation, insulation and shading from a retained chestnut tree allow passive solar gain and simple heat exchange to keep the house warm even on the coldest day.

80 Ecohome, Cumberland Basin, 1996
Bruges Tozer Partnership

The Ecohome is, by contrast, a demonstration project: in effect a library of techniques and working equipment which can be used to make new or existing houses more environmentally friendly, and in particular more energy-efficient. The design, which won a city council competition, is (as at Redland) oriented to maximise solar gain and flow of warm air through the building. It is designed to link by bridge into the council's green demonstration centre, Create, in the adjacent historic warehouse.

Ecohouse, ↗
Redland *(79)*
26 Grove Road,
Redland, BS6
CLIENT
Turlough New Homes
ARCHITECT
Exedra D S Drage
Architects
STRUCTURAL ENGINEER
John Taylor
MECHANICAL AND
ELECTRICAL ENGINEER
David Young
MAIN CONTRACTOR
Turlough New Homes

Ecohome, →
Cumberland Basin *(80)*
Create, B Bond,
Smeaton Road, BS1
CLIENT
Bristol City Council
ARCHITECT
Bruges Tozer Partnership
CONSULTANT ENGINEER
Buro Happold, Bath
QUANTITY SURVEYOR
Stephens & Co, Bath
MAIN CONTRACTOR
Bristol City Council
Contract Services

81 Goldney Hall student residences, 1996
Alec French Partnership

Goldney Hall student residences centre on the 18th-century
Goldney House with its superb gardens and grotto. In the 1960s
Architects Co-Partnership designed an annexe of study bedrooms
west of and below the main gardens, which won awards but
proved too small and came to seem too sharp an intrusion. Alec
French Partnership convinced a sceptical planning authority that
their scheme for recladding the ACP buildings and infilling
between them could actually enhance the backdrop to the gardens.
It does. Its balconies and belvederes have an oriental lightness; its
landscaped courtyards are a delight.

Goldney →
residences *(81)*
Lower Clifton Hill,
Clifton, BS8
CLIENT
University of Bristol
ARCHITECT
Alec French Partnership
QUANTITY SURVEYOR
Gleeds, Bristol
CONSULTANT ENGINEER
Whitby & Bird, London
LANDSCAPE ARCHITECT
Balston & Co, Devizes
MAIN CONTRACTOR
Laing South-West

82 Bristol Zoo: Canopy and Restaurant, 1992
Peter Ware

Historic buildings, the need to give wild animals more natural living environments, and an ever more demanding public - these factors conflict and pose severe problems for a late 20th zoo. Bristol Zoo has been fortunate to be headed by a president - Peter Floyd - who is also an architect. Not all the changes of the last 10 years have been welcomed by his fellow architects, but two buildings at least have evoked widespread acclaim.

Peter Ware's refurbishment and extension of the zoo's 1930s restaurant building gives one-third more room (new kitchens and thus a larger eating area). A large and graceful tented structure provides sheltered outdoor space, a focus for activity, and a stronger connection between the inside and outside spaces.

83 Bristol Zoo: Entrance Building, 1996
LMP Architects

LMP's main entrance building meets the need for a welcoming, sheltered entrance while respecting the two listed 19th-century lodges. Glass walled and with a pyramidal roof, it provides a more spacious foyer for ticket sales and information as well as a "window" into the zoo grounds. The lodges were converted to house shops, toilets and other facilities. The present overcrowded sales function is a temporary aberration and should soon find a new location.

Bristol Zoo: Canopy →
and Restaurant (82)
Clifton Down, BS8
CLIENT
President and Council of
Bristol Zoo Gardens
ARCHITECT
Peter Ware
QUANTITY SURVEYOR
Martin Ryder,
Gloucestershire
STRUCTURAL ENGINEER
Ian Duncan, Bristol
MAIN CONTRACTOR
Caines Construction Ltd

Bristol Zoo: Entrance ↘
Building (83)
Clifton Down, BS8
CLIENT
President and Council of
Bristol Zoo Gardens
ARCHITECT
LMP Architects
QUANTITY SURVEYOR
WPE Ltd, Bristol
STRUCTURAL,
MECHANICAL AND
ELECTRICAL CONSULTANT
Whitby & Bird, Bath
PLANNING SUPERVISOR
BGP, Bristol
MAIN CONTRACTOR
Caines Construction Ltd,
Bristol

84 The Beeches, 1996
Peter Ware

This is the recycling of a recycled house. In the 1960s someone built the very dull, horizontal detached house (right) on the foundations of something considerably older. Peter and Marie Ware  liked the site but not the house; the planners gave permission for a rebuilding within the confines of what was there, and Peter transformed it: an architect working for the most demanding of clients, himself and his wife. It is a house in tune with its surroundings, properly reticent at the front, more outward going at the back with longer views and an eccentric, half-octagon conservatory; and with a part open-plan, part double-height interior. Every detail of the interior is his, including staircase, bannisters and doors. The Beeches is one of the most interesting creations of an architect most valued by, and now most missed by his friends - and to whom this book is dedicated.

The Beeches *(84)*
Manor Road, Abbots
Leigh, BS8
CLIENT
Mr & Mrs Peter Ware
ARCHITECT
Peter Ware
STRUCTURAL ENGINEER
Ian Duncan
CONTRACTOR
Bob Bennett

85 Bengough House, 1997
Feilden Clegg Architects

Bengough House is a dual nursing and residential home built at Brentry to replace the original home built in 1878 with funds left for the purpose by Alderman Bengough; that location at Horfield Road had become unsuitable. Bristol Municipal Charities wanted, and were able to afford, a high-quality building with generous space standards in both the 40 bedrooms and communal spaces.

But the new site - at the junction of two busy roads - posed some problems. That is why, from the street, it looks somewhat fortress-like: solid brick and stone form a barrier to noise, and the spaces immediately behind these two elevations are mostly corridors, bathrooms and offices.

The timber-clad, garden-front is altogether more open and welcoming; this is where the 40 rooms are, arranged in two L-shaped, two-storey wings. Each bedsitter has its own toilet and washing facilities, but residents share a kitchen/living room area with others in a "family group" of 10. Here residents can not only look out on the garden, but also sit out on their own patios and balconies. The glazed main entrance, recessed between protecting barrier blocks, leads into a light, spacious double-height hall; this in turn extends into a south-facing garden room.

↑ **Bengough House** (85)
Crow Lane,
← Brentry, BS10
CLIENT
Orchard Homes (Bristol Municipal Charities)
ARCHITECT
Feilden Clegg Architects
QUANTITY SURVEYOR
WPE
STRUCTURAL ENGINEER
Whitby & Bird
MECHANICAL AND
ELECTRICAL CONSULTANT
Halcrow Gilbert
LANDSCAPE ARCHITECT
Peter Thoday Associates
MAIN CONTRACTOR
Stansell Builders Ltd

86 Vision Care Centre, 1993
Alec French Partnership

Bristol Royal Society for the Blind is the oldest charity of its kind in Britain, having provided facilities and support for visually handicapped people for two centuries. The starting point for the architects was a recognition that the common condition is visual impairment rather than total blindness (a rarity). Consequently light and colour are both important in this building - the less vision you have, the more you value them.

The BRSB's purpose was to bring together under one roof a variety of previously fragmented services for visually impaired people. These include its own services - rehabilitation and training programmes, tape and Braille publications, information and displays of useful aids and equipment - but also regional centres for the Royal National Institute for the Blind and for the Guide Dogs for the Blind Association. This last includes a special kennel block. The building also includes meeting rooms and a small conference hall with kitchen.

In default of comprehensive published guidelines, the architects undertook a series of visits accompanied by BRSB officials and blind and visually impaired people. The result is a building which goes behind cliches and stereotypes and to the heart of sight-impaired people's real needs. Colour contrasts in such things as handrails and power switches, and increased natural or artificial light at "crossroads" in the circulation system aim to give maximum clarity of direction, reinforcing the colour contrast of tactile floor pads at these focal points. Ground floor corridors gain extra light from translucent panels in peripheral offices; first floor corridors from glazing at the roof ridge. The whole ambience is of welcoming light and colour.

Planting round the outside of the building concentrates on sweet-smelling species like honeysuckle and jasmine. The siting of the centre in a down-at-heel inner city area of Bedminster has three advantages: a lower price for the site; easy access by bus, on which most users are dependent; and a boost for inner city regeneration. The complex includes a bungalow for the resident caretaker; perhaps thanks to this there has been next to no vandalism.

Vision Care ↑
Centre (86)
Stillhouse Lane,
Bedminster, BS3
CLIENTS
Bristol Royal Society for
the Blind/Guide Dogs for
the Blind Association
ARCHITECT
Alec French Partnership
QUANTITY SURVEYOR
Colin Jenkins
Partnership, Bristol
STRUCTURAL ENGINEER
Kenneth Brown &
Partners, Bristol
SERVICES ENGINEER
WSP Parson Brown,
Bristol
MAIN CONTRACTOR
Trafalgar House
Construction (Regions)

87 Orlebar Gardens affordable housing, 1995 and 1997
Percy Thomas Partnership

In an area of drab public housing, 1950s Orlebar Gardens was sick both physically and socially. PTP stripped it down, cured its damp and condensation problems, added lifts and pitched roofs, reclad and brightened its external appearance. The 56-flat Orlebar complex with its internal courtyard garden became an attractive and safe environment which gave the people who lived there a fresh start. The ultimate tribute: many passers-by think Orlebar is new, private housing.

↑ **Orlebar Gardens** (87)
Orlebar Gardens,
Lawrence Weston, BS11
CLIENT AND OWNER
Bristol City Council
ARCHITECT
Percy Thomas Partnership
(Architects) Ltd
QUANTITY SURVEYOR
Symonds
STRUCTURAL ENGINEER
Clarke Bond Partnership

**MECHANICAL AND
ELECTRICAL ENGINEER**
Hoare Lea & partners
LANDSCAPE ARCHITECT
Bristol City Council
Leisure Services
MAIN CONTRACTOR
Laing Construction;
Tarmac Contract
Housing

Housing for →
Vietnamese
refugees *(88)*
164-166, Cheltenham
Road, Montpelier, BS6
CLIENT
Bristol Churches Housing
Association acting for An
Viet Housing Association
ARCHITECT
Beardsworth Gallanaugh
& Partners
QUANTITY SURVEYOR
Colin Jenkins Partnership
STRUCTURAL ENGINEER
Jenkins & Potter
LANDSCAPE ARCHITECT
The Appleton Group
MAIN CONTRACTOR
William Cowlin, Bristol

88 Housing for Vietnamese refugees, 1995
Beardsworth Gallanaugh & Partners

Refugees in a strange city and an alien culture are vulnerable; they often need a protective home environment. Bristol Churches Housing Association, which has a commendable track record in inner city housing, acted for An Viet, which is now the owner. The site was not an easy one: a large semi-detached late Victorian villa fronting Cheltenham Road, but behind it a disused builder's yard, dotted with odd buildings, surrounded by a teeteringly high brick wall, with, beneath it and close to the surface, a large 19th-century brick culvert carrying Cutler's Brook. Access to the yard was a narrow lane.

BGP converted the house into a maisonette and three flats. That was the easy part. Then, by using lightweight (and energy efficient) timber-frame construction, they contrived to fit eight mostly three-storey homes round the courtyard: five sizeable family houses (extended families are a common pattern among Vietnamese); one small starter home; and a large maisonette with a flat attached, which could be combined. The courtyard form is popular with residents and reinforces their sense of community; the colour-rendered walls and low-pitched, overhanging slate roofs with bracketed eaves aimed to reflect the Regency character of the adjoining Montpelier conservation area.

← **QEH Theatre** (89)
Berkeley Place,
Clifton, BS8
CLIENT
Queen Elizabeth Hospital
ARCHITECT
Moxley Jenner Ltd
QUANTITY SURVEYOR
WPE Ltd
STRUCTURAL ENGINEER
MRM
ELECTRICAL AND
MECHANICAL CONSULTANT
Ferguson & Partners
CONTRACTOR
Wilkins & Coventry

89 QEH Theatre, 1990
Moxley Jenner Ltd

A difficult site, in townscape terms, in terrain and in size. Queen Elizabeth's Hospital wanted a theatre for the school's own drama productions and to be available for letting to outside productions, but it had to be squeezed into a tiny, steeply sloping site below Brandon Hill and between QEH's 1840s battlemented neo-Elizabethan buildings and Georgian terraces to the east. Moxley Jenner's solution works well both visually and functionally.

The flexible 250-seat auditorium, internally a sort of irregular octagon, is at first floor level, thus reducing the need to excavate into the hillside. Horizontal banding of yellow and brown bricks catch the colour tones of both groups of neighbouring buildings. Stairs, circulation and foyer fit into a glazed drum, communicating with the street at ground floor and the school grounds at first floor level. A droll little 1840s sally-port with mock portcullis is retained and helps with the visual adjustment. But it is the skilful choice and assured handling of materials and forms which makes this building such a successful addition to the Clifton townscape.

Old Vic Theatre →
**School Dance
Studio** (90)
Pembroke Road,
Clifton, BS8
CLIENT
Bristol Old Vic
Theatre School
ARCHITECT
Ferguson Mann Architects
QUANTITY SURVEYOR
Mildred Howells & Co
STRUCTURAL ENGINEER
Whitby & Bird, Bath
ELECTRICAL CONSULTANT
Control Electrical
Installations
LANDSCAPE ARCHITECT
Lawrence & Wrightson,
London
MAIN CONTRACTOR
Stone & Co, Bristol

90 Old Vic Theatre School: new Dance Studio, 1995
Ferguson Mann Architects

The Old Vic Theatre School occupied a pair of Victorian semi-detached villas plus extension which filled nearly half the garden. But even large Victorian rooms do not provide all the spaces needed by a theatre school: for instance, room for one dance student to stand on another's shoulders with headroom for further upward movement. Yet this was a prominent street corner in a conservation area. For the school to have a new multi-purpose space, an ingenious and imaginative solution was needed.

The architects looked around and saw that Clifton's Victorian houses often had rather grand conservatories, sometimes gothic, sometimes classical. The dance studio reinter-prets that idea, but without any historicist frills. The studio needed to be raised above ground to allow access to existing workshops, so why not, they reasoned, show the public what went on inside? With their structural engineers, they created what is in effect a jumbo-sized but beautifully detailed glass and steel display case.

But theatre and dance students need to be able to control the microclimate in which they work, so high-level louvres provide ventilation; the trees and brise-soleil control solar gain; and ceiling heating panels plus concealed fan-assisted convectors keep them warm. And, when the trees are not too fully in leaf, students can get used to an audience of passers-by. The building borrows from the character of Clifton, reinterprets it, and, far from damaging the conservation area, positively enhances it.

91 Spike Island Centre, 1998
Niall Phillips Architects

This 1960s building was purpose-built for Brooke Bond as a machine for unloading, blending, and packaging tea. The tea chests came in at one end, were conveyed to the first floor for unloading, progressed westward for blending, westward again down chutes to fill tea bags or packets. The whole shape and configuration of the building was so specific that, when Brooke Bond no longer wanted it, few people could see any sensible re-use.

But about that time Artspace, a charitable trust providing working space for young (and not-so-young) artists, was becoming desperate for somewhere to replace the crumbling, cramped rabbit-warren of a warehouse they then occupied. Niall Phillips Architects demonstrated that the Brooke Bond building could be made to suit their purpose. It does so surprisingly well.

The first floor of its eastern end, where the opening of tea-chests went on under a spectacular switchback roof, is divided into flexible, subdivisible ply-walled studio spaces, with corridors under the low points of the roof and studios benefiting from the top-lit highs; the double-height hall where packing took place under a barrel vault lit by glass bricks in a concrete grid, was a ready-made exhibition hall; the gallery is neatly and economically screened off using cheap, very 1960s glazing panels. You know you've seen them before, but something's different. Yes, they're used horizontally instead of vertically. Other spaces accommodate the heavy industry end of the fine arts, like welding and metal fabrication; further spaces are let out to arts-type companies to achieve financial viability.

When to their surprise Artspace and NPA heard they'd won a full lottery grant, it might have been said, "Their cup runneth over". Alas! Between the good news and their securing possession of the building, the vandals moved in, stripping away wiring and pipes. To gain a few hundred pounds' worth of metal, they did £400,000 of damage. So instead of a de luxe conversion, Artspace had to accept an austerity job. It still worked very well - perhaps in some ways better. And just recently there has been another sizeable hiccup: the glass bricks over the exhibition space have shown an alarming tendency to fall out of a crumbling concrete grid. NPA are mulling over effective, low-cost solutions.

Spike Island →
Centre (91)
Cumberland Road,
Spike Island, BS1
CLIENT
Artspace, Bristol
ARCHITECT
Niall Phillips Architects
CONSULTANT ARTISTS
Louise Barber, John
O'Connor
QUANTITY SURVEYOR
WPE
STRUCTURAL ENGINEER
Hyder Consulting
SERVICES ENGINEER
Integrated Design
Partnership
MAIN CONTRACTOR
Stansell

92 Public art in Castle Park, 1993
Bristol City Council

This site, once occupied by the Saxons and later by a Norman castle, was long the commercial heart of Bristol until flattened by bombs in 1940. Creation of a park was the subject of designs by the eminent landscape architect Dame Sylvia Crowe, some parts of which are still visible. The opportunity to create a high quality city park came in 1998 with the income from a temporary car park during nearby shopping redevelopment.

The city then used this money for an imaginative scheme involving both its own landscape architects and a group of artists whose specially commissioned works form part of the park landscape. These included wooden seats of distinctive but comfortable design, railings, ornamental steel balustrades to a footbridge and many others. The works pictured here are a drinking fountain adorned with such symbolic Bristol features as a boat, a castle and tobacco leaves by Kate Malone; and *Beside the Still Waters*, an avenue of pleached lime-trees with hornbeam hedges leading to a huge pineapple-like sculpture set in a spiral of water and stone by Peter Randall-Page in collaboration with city council landscape architects.

← **Public art in Castle Park** *(92)*
↙ Wine Street, BS1
CLIENT
Bristol City Council
PUBLIC ART CONSULTANT
Lesley Greene
LANDSCAPE ARCHITECTS
Martin Deaville, Alex Fraser (Bristol City Council Leisure Services)
PROJECT MANAGER
Jon Wheatley
CO-ORDINATOR, HISTORY AND INTERPRETATION
Gillian Dawson
MAIN CONTRACTOR FOR PARK
Trafalgar House
ARTIST, DRINKING FOUNTAIN
Kate Malone
ARTIST, BESIDE THE STILL WATERS:
Peter Randall-Page

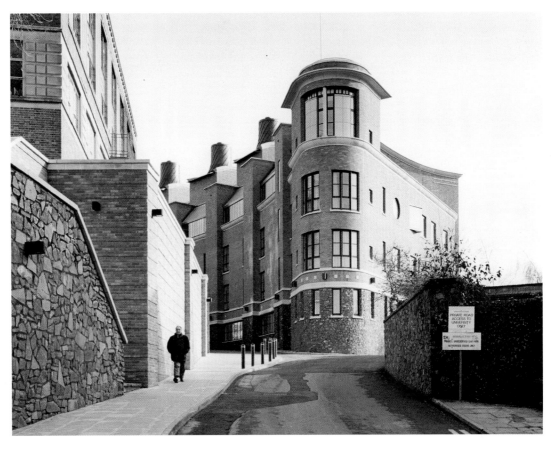

Synthetic ↑
Chemistry *(93)* ↗
Cantocks Close,
Clifton, BS8
CLIENT
University of Bristol
ARCHITECT
Percy Thomas Partnership
QUANTITY SURVEYOR
Gleeds
ENGINEERING CONSULTANT
Ove Arup & Partners
LANDSCAPE DESIGN
University External Works
Department
MAIN CONTRACTOR
Wates Construction

93 University of Bristol Synthetic Chemistry Building, 1999
Percy Thomas Partnership

This new building high on a hillside at the heart of the main University site goes some way to realise Sir George Oatley's dream of a ring of towers. It follows the sweeping curve of the steep hillside; its external walls use biscuit-coloured brick above a plinth of local and reconstituted stone; its main elevation alternates glazed vertical bays with projecting solid sections which look like towers, and above this rise four black, lead-clad chimneys: these accommodate flues to carry away fumes from 16 new teaching laboratories. Reminiscent of ship's funnels, they make a dramatic contribution to the skyline.

To complete the building the University wanted, to a tight timetable and on budget, architects, project managers, engineers and cost controllers used an innovative contract and all worked together under one roof with client and contractors to cut delays and ensure "buildability".

121

8 Millennium landmarks

By 1992, the Lloyds headquarters had shown that landmark development on the wasteland of Canons Marsh was viable; the need now was to show how comfortable, stimulating places for people and entertainment could be extended westwards from Watershed, and without being swamped by roads, cars and car parks. Four of Bristol's most enterprising architects combined resources in the Concept Planning Group (CPG), and found a backer in Bristol's Chamber of Commerce and Initiative, which in turn won the support of the City Council.

The CPG produced an urban design strategy for Harbourside (as Canon's Marsh now became); competitions brought leading British and international architects for three key buildings. Two of them have been built; the third, Behnisch's stunning performing arts centre, fell victim to a funding squeeze, but - exceptionally - merits recording as a brilliant design, a lost opportunity and, perhaps, London-biased funding policies which give too little weight to the needs of regional centres in what promises to be an era of devolved government.

← **Harbourside Centre** (94)
Harbourside, Canon's Marsh, BS1
Behnisch, Behnisch & Partner
STRUCTURAL ENGINEER
Buro Happold
QUANTITY SURVEYOR
Gleeds
SERVICES ENGINEER
Max Fordham
THEATRE CONSULTANT
Theatre Projects
ACOUSTIC CONSULTAN
Muller BBM

94 Harbourside Centre, abortive
Behnisch, Behnisch & Partner

For once, Bristol seemed to be doing everything right. The proposal was for a centre for the performing arts, replacing the Colston Hall's sub-standard facilities with a new 2,000-seat concert hall and also providing a dance theatre and three further spaces for a programme of community education. The location - on the waterside between the Lloyds building and Watershed - was one which would have maximum impact, both visually and for urban regeneration; the use was one which would draw people to the area. Choice of architect was by international competition, backed by a National Lottery proposal developed to the point where the Arts Council was ready to give funding for the whole design process; and a team of specialist consultants worked with the chosen architect, the client and prospective users to develop the final design.

Behnisch's latest design, at the time when the Arts Council pulled the plug, promised to be a superb landmark building. Its complex external geometry must to a large extent have reflected the challenge of fitting uses and circulation spaces into a very tight site. The large areas of glazing, particularly on the waterside elevation, were calculated to show the building in use alive with people - sitting, standing, eating, drinking, moving along and up and down foyers and stairs and ramps - an effect which at night would have been dramatic. The design sent clear messages about transparency and accessibility; the client wished to break down the cultural apartheid that made "the Arts" unapproachable by a large part of the population, especially young people. The way in which the upper part of the building projected out over the quayside allowed it to signal its presence to passers-by in The Centre: it would have been a visible symbol of the renaissance of the whole Canons Marsh/ Harbourside area.

**Millennium
Square** *(95)*
Harbourside, BS1
CLIENT
@t Bristol
DESIGNER
Concept Planning Group
LANDSCAPE ARCHITECT
Michael Balston
ENGINEERING CONSULTANT
Ove Arup & Partners
QUANTITY SURVEYOR
Davis Langdon & Everest
PROJECT MANAGER
Symonds
CONTRACTOR
Tarmac Ltd

95 Millennium Square, 2000
Concept Planning Group

In spite of the loss of the Behnisch building, Harbourside is emerging as a lively and attractive new quarter, with strong links to other parts of the city centre. This is in large measure thanks to the CPG, a forward-thinking planning and design consortium made up of architects from two Bristol practices, Ferguson Mann Architects and Alec French Partnership, with another, James Bruges, as its original consultant. This group not only provided the overall strategy; they also designed Harbourside's focal point, Millennium Square - a pedestrian space with parking hidden away underground - as well as the Millennium Mile and other tree-lined, landscaped public spaces. CPG's contribution ensures that Harbourside is more than just a collection of buildings, that it is a real place.

Millennium Square is just the largest of a whole chain of public spaces designed (a) as a pedestrian-friendly whole, (b) with new and old buildings integrated into the overall design, and (c) with public art used imaginatively to animate and interpret places and spaces. Millennium Square itself - 6,500 sq metres, or as large as Parliament Square in London - is conceived as a space where people will gather, rendezvous, eat and drink at cafés and listen to music. Its most prominent piece of public art is William Pye's Aquarena, an impressive arrangement of flooded terraces and archways of water you can walk through. The square also has an Analemma, a light feature with a time theme by David Ward; and even in the car park under the square, artists Tim Noble and Sue Webster make their contribution with words in constantly changing patterns of lights on a background of stainless steel.

In Anchor Place, in front of Chris Wilkinson's Explore @t Bristol building, scientific discovery is celebrated by Simon Thomas's fragmented cone, recognising the Nobel Prize winning work on anti-matter of Bristolian physicist Paul Dirac; in Anchor Square near Michael Hopkins' Wildscreen a striking sculpture representing the rhinoceros beetle is planned. @t Bristol has also commissioned representational work, including statues of historical figures - Thomas Chatterton, the boy poet; William Penn, founder of Pennsylvania; William Tyndale, 16th-century translator of the bible - from sculptor Lawrence Holofcener.

96 Pero's Bridge, 1999
Eilis O'Connell, Ove Arup & Partners

Pero's Bridge *(96)*
linking Harbourside and
Narrow Quay, BS1
CLIENT
JT Group in partnership
with Bristol City Council
SCULPTOR
Eilis O'Connell
STRUCTURAL ENGINEER
Ove Arup & Partners
QUANTITY SURVEYOR
Banks Wood & Partners
FABRICATOR
David Abel
CONSTRUCTION ON SITE
Dew Construction

This footbridge across St Augustine's Reach provides a key link in a new and already very well used pedestrian route between Harbourside and the Arnolfini/Queen Square/King Street area. With its distinctive "horns" rising above its supporting "central" pier, it has become surprisingly quickly one of Bristol's best-known landmarks. In fact, that pier - the structure rising from the river-bed from which the opening central section hinges — is not itself central, which makes the bridge look at first lopsided when seen from up- or down-stream. But it works, visually as well as functionally.

The design of Pero's Bridge, by sculptor Eilis O'Connell and structural engineers Ove Arup & Partners, is intended as a gesture of atonement by Bristol for the slave trade which enriched it in the 18th and early 19th centuries. This dark strand in the city's history was marked in 1999 by a no-punches-pulled but remarkably objective exhibition, "A Respectable trade? Bristol and Transatlantic Slavery", at the City Museum; while the bridge itself was said to symbolise "a bridge across the centuries" between Queen Square, noble architecture built with the proceeds of slavery, and the new, hopefully more enlightened world of the 21st century represented by Wildscreen and Explore @t Bristol.

The Pero who gives his name to the bridge was, of course, a slave: one of 438 transported in 1762 in horrific conditions by the Bristol merchantman *Black Prince*. More than 40 died on the voyage. It is right that Bristol should make this gesture.

**Wildscreen @t Bristol
2000** *(97)*
Anchor Square,
Harbourside, BS1
CLIENT
@t Bristol
ARCHITECT
Michael Hopkins &
Partners
PROJECT MANAGERS
Symonds
QUANTITY SURVEYOR
Davis Langdon &
Everest
ENGINEERING
CONSULTANTS
Buro Happold acoustic
CONSULTANT
Sandy Brown Associates
CONSTRUCTION MANAGER
Bovis Ltd

97 Wildscreen @t Bristol, 2000
Michael Hopkins & Partners

This project starts from a recognition that 95% of animal species are smaller than a hen's egg, yet make a contribution to Earth's well-being out of all proportion to their size and visibility. These are the stars of the show at Wildscreen. The building which displays and explains them has five main parts: a 19th-century leadworks at the south end of the site; a large, windowless IMAX theatre at its north end; and in between them entrance foyer,

Botanical House and exhibition galleries.

The restored leadworks, freed of later additions, houses shop, café and offices. The entrance foyer links these to the Botanical House, a huge, sunny conservatory planted in zones linking with the adjacent exhibition galleries. These provide the "black box" environment and large, flexible, well-serviced floors needed by an electronic zoo. Hopkins' aim has been to express the form and construction of each of these elements but bring them together in a coherent and legible way.

Explore @t Bristol *(98)*
Anchor Square,
Harbourside, BS1
CLIENT
Explore @t Bristol
ARCHITECT
Chris Wilkinson
Architects
PROJECT MANAGER
Symonds
QUANTITY SURVEYOR
Davis Langdon & Everest
ENGINEERING CONSULTANT
Ove Arup & Partners
LANDSCAPE ARCHITECT
CPC
CONSTRUCTION MANAGER
Symonds Wolf

98 Explore @t Bristol, 2000
Chris Wilkinson Architects

Explore @t Bristol is the first of a new generation of hands-on science centres. Appropriately it converts and extends an existing building of some importance in the history of 20th-century technology: the listed Hennibique concrete goods shed built in 1903 for the Great Western Railway. The enlargement - upwards and sideways - is in steel and glass, but the cladding is set back on two sides to create an arcade.

From the first floor gallery a bridge leads to the planetarium, housed in a striking 16m- diameter sphere clad in stainless steel. A gallery added to the north facade has a full-height glazed wall whose "intelligent glass systems" and special lighting effects respond both to passers-by and environmental conditions.

99 Reviving The Centre, 2000
Concept Planning Group

Photos taken in the late 19th-century at what is now The Centre show not the present traffic maelstrom but water, quays and ships. Bristol is now poised, with National Lottery support, to bring back something of that magical mix of water, buildings, people and activity. The River Froom, alas, stays underground, but traffic is curbed and the pedestrian's lot greatly improved. Above the river's course an avenue of trees, a line of moving water and ten Millennium Beacons, by light artist Martin Richman, march down to St Augustine's Reach to recreate symbolically the link between Froom and Floating Harbour. Other features include steps down from the tree-lined promenade to a new landing stage, a waterside café-restaurant, and the resiting from Canon's Marsh of Ferguson Mann's striking display structure.

← **The Centre** (99)
Reviving The
Centre, 2000
CLIENT
@t Bristol
ARCHITECT
Concept Planning Group
QUANTITY SURVEYOR
Davis Langdon & Everest
ENGINEER
City Council Health &
Environmental Services
PROJECT MANAGER
Symonds
MAIN CONTRACTOR
C J Pearce & Co Ltd

Queen Square *(100)* ↑
Queen Square, City
Centre, BS1
CLIENT
Bristol City Council
ARCHITECT
City Council City Centre
Projects and Urban
Design
PRESENTATION DRAWINGS
Niall Phillips

QUANTITY SURVEYOR
Davis Langdon & Everest
ENGINEER
City Council, Health &
Environmental Services

100 Queen Square restored, 2000-2002
Bristol City Council Centre Projects

One of Bristol's grandest spaces, Queen Square was wrecked in the
1930s when the City Council ran a dual carriageway diagonally
across it. In the mid-90s they closed that road. Now, with Lottery
money, the city and its partner property owners are to restore the
central space, move cars out of the forecourts of the houses,
generally lessen the impact of parked vehicles, and make this once
more a gracious, tranquil public space.

Envoi: into the 21st century

Putting together this book has been very much a process of shooting at a moving target. The general approach has been to exclude what has not yet been built, but the "Millennium works" in Chapter 8 seemed to us so important that they demanded inclusion. They also point towards a welcome change in Bristol's attitude to new architecture and urban design: bold, comprehensive, and having the 'end users', the public, very much in mind and involved. The willingness of councillors to think again about the leisure development on the west side of New World Square is in this respect most welcome.

The signs, then, are more hopeful. Bristol's historic built environment is appreciated and defended more resolutely and determinedly than probably ever before; the public, the city council and property owners are showing a new awareness of what can be achieved in creating not only good buildings but good built environments, which include but are more than just the buildings. The penny has dropped: good public places make a city popular with people, and this has - to put it crudely - a huge commercial pay-off. The old Victorian ethic of enlightened self-interest is finding new expression.

But acceptance of these ideas in principle is one thing, delivering the tangible results quite another. It requires continuous and intelligent vigilance by the Civic Society and other groups and individuals; and creative, lateral thinking by design professionals, both inside and outside the local planning authority. There is a case for saying that every city should have a Concept Planning Group or something like it; and that it should not necessarily be an ad hoc, limited-life exercise. The CPG or something like it will be needed in the coming century, after its current commissions are completed, as a complement and stimulus to the official planning apparatus.

The fact that improvements to the city centre may seem to have been substantially achieved does not mean there is no pressing role for creative urban design. The focus could usefully turn to local centres in need of upgrading and rethinking. Many of the losses and environmental disasters of post-war redevelopment have come about from failure to see and appreciate what exists and how it could be improved. New political imperatives such as improved public transport and social inclusion should go hand in hand with unblinkered appraisal of what we have and imaginative but practicable proposals for improvement and renewal.

Acknowledgements

This book could not have been written without the help of the very many people who went to often considerable trouble to provide or check information. They include, of course, many of the owners or occupiers of buildings included, as well as architects and other professionals, all of whom are credited in the captions to the pictures. I also owe an incalculable debt to the authors of the works listed in the bibliography below. Theirs in many cases was the original labour of research; I have often been happy to adopt their choices and judgements. To all these sources my thanks; they are not responsible for my errors.

A few of the pictures are not by John Trelawny-Ross - chiefly those of buildings or places not yet completed when we went to press. The exception is the photo of the Brabazon Assembly Hall which appears courtesy of British Aerospace Airbus plc. Pictures of New World Square, Anchor Square, Explore @t Bristol, and Wildscreen @t Bristol were provided by @t Bristol; those of The Centre and Queen Square come courtesy of the City Council; those of two abortive schemes, the Harbourside Centre and housing at Wapping Wharf, courtesy of their respective architects.

The book would also not have been published without all those organisations and individuals who provided "money up-front" as sponsors or subscribers. We are particularly grateful to the University of Bristol and Bristol City Council; also to the sponsors, whose names are listed on page 2.

My special thanks go to the Architecture Centre, its former director Sasha Lubetkin, its present director Mark Pearson, and their staff; to its chairman David Mellor who has done a terrific job raising the money; and to our publisher John Sansom for his confidence, support and expertise; and to him and his wife Angela for hospitality and good company.

Books consulted

Aldous, Tony: *Changing Bristol; New Architecture and Conservation 1960-1980*, Redcliffe Press, 1980.
Burrough, T H B: *City Buildings Series - Bristol*, Studio Vista, 1970.
Mallory, Keith: *The Bristol House*, Redcliffe Press, 1985
Mowl, Tim: *Bristol: Last Age of the Merchant Princes*, Millstream Books, 1991.
Punter, John V: *Design Control in Bristol, 1940-1990*, Redcliffe Press, 1990.
Gomme, Andor; Jenner, Michael; Little, Bryan: *Bristol: An Architectural History*, Lund Humphries, 1979.

Index of buildings and places

Abbots Leigh - The Beeches *110-111*

Architecture Centre *105*

Avon Street - Marketing Centre *104*

Aztec West *90-91*

BBC Regional Headquarters *75*

B-Bond Warehouse *25*

Bedminster - Vision Care Centre *6, 114*

Bedminster Down - Bristol Water HQ *47*

    Pavilions (former CEGB) *67*

Bond Street - Spectrum *74*

Brabazon Assembly Hall *42*

Bradley Stoke - RAC Supercentre *84-85*

Brentry - Bengough House *112-113*

Bridewell Street *69*

Bristol Crown Court *87*

Bristol Royal Infirmary *16*

Bristol Zoo - Canopy and Restaurant
    108-109

    Entrance Building *108*

Broad Street - Everard's Printing works *17*

Cabot Café *18*

Canon's Marsh, see Harbourside

Castle Park - public art/ landscape *120*

Centre, The *130*

Cheese Lane - Shot Tower *46*

Christmas Steps *70-71*

Churches - All Saints Church *49*

    Clifton Cathedral *62-63*

    St Bernadette's *50*

    St Edyth's Church *35*

Clifton - All Saints Church *49*

    BBC headquarters *75*

    RC Cathedral *62-63*

Garden Court, Alma Vale Road *80*

Goldney residences *107*

Old Vic Theatre School *118*

QEH Theatre *117*

Stonewest House, Oakfield Grove *79*

College Green - Cabot Café *18*

    Central Library *14-15*

    Council House *33*

    landscape restoration *86-87*

Colston Avenue - Colston Centre *64*

    former Electricity Offices *30*

    Northcliffe House *30*

Colston Street - Colston House *31*

    conservation *70-71*

Commercial Road, Redcliffe - City council
    flats *39*

Corn Street - Fresco Italian Brasserie *37*

Cotham - former Homeopathic Hospital
    12-13

    Western Congregational College *11*

Council House *33*

Cribbs Causeway, The Mall *9, 92-93*

Cumberland Road - Spike Island Centre *119*

Electricity Offices, former *30*

Everard's Printing Works *17*

Explore @t Bristol *129*

Filton - Brabazon Assembly Hall *42*

Flax Bourton - Five Houses *59*

Frenchay - Manor Park Estate *47*

Great George Street *73*

Harbourside *8, 122-129*

    Anchor Place *125*

Explore @t Bristol *129*

Harbourside Centre *8, 123*

Lloyds Bank HQ *83*

Millennium Square *124*

Pero's Bridge *126-127*

Watershed *78-79*

Wildscreen *128*

Hartcliffe - Wills complex *65*

Homeopathic Hospital, former *12-13*

Horsefair - Lewis's (Bentall's) department
    store *40-41*

Hotwells - Poole's Wharf *103*

Housing - The Beeches, Abbots Leigh *110-111*

    Bengough House *113*

    Carfax Court *77*

    Concrete House *32*

    Downs Park East *22*

    Ecohome, Cumberland Basin *106*

    Ecohouse, Redland *106*

    Flax Bourton houses *59*

    Garden Court *80*

    High Kingsdown *58-59*

    Lodge Street *53-55*

    Manor Park estate *47*

    Orlebar Gardens *6, 115*

    Pitch & Pay Span estate *48*

    Poole's Wharf *103*

    Redcliffe Flats *39*

    Vietnamese refugees, housing for *116*

    WCA Warehouse conversion *96-97*

Jamaica Street Carriage Works *18-19*

Kingsdown - High Kingsdown *58-59*

Lawrence Weston - Orlebar Gardens *115*
Lewis's department store *40-41*
Leigh Woods - White House *21*
Library, Central *14-15*
Lockleaze Secondary School *43*
Lodge Street - repair and renewal *53-55*
Lower Maudlin Street - Eye Hospital
    sculpture *81*

Marketing & Exhibition Centre *104*
Marlborough Hill, Bristol Royal Infirmary *16*
Ministry of Defence Procurement Executive
    88-89
Montpelier - Vietnamese housing *116*

Narrow Quay - Architecture Centre *105*
Newspaper offices - Bristol Times & Mirror
    (former) *24*
    Bristol United Press *60*
    Northcliffe House *30*

Office buildings -Bridewell Street *69*
    Bristol Water *47*
    Centre Gate House *70*
    Colston Centre *64*
    Great George Street *73*
    Lloyds Bank Headquarters *83*
    Pavilions (formerly CEGB) *67*
    RAC Supercentre *84-85*
    Redcliff Street (Robinson building) *45*
    Redcliffe Quay *98-99*
    St Augustine's Court *72-73*
    St Bartholemew's *70-71*
    St James's Court *94-95*
    Scottish Life Building *61*
    Spectrum *74-75*
    Stonewest House *79*
    Wessex House *66*
Old Market - conservation and renewal
    56-57

Old Vic Theatre School Dance Studio *118*

Passage Street - Wessex House *51*
Pero's Bridge *126-127*
Public art - Brick Sculpture, Bristol Eye
    Hospital *81*
    Castle Park *120*
Public spaces - Anchor Place *125*
    Castle Park *120*
    College Green *86*
    Centre, The *130*
    New World Square *124*
    Queen Square *131*

Queens Road - Wills Memorial Building *27*
Queen Square *7, 131*
QEH Theatre *117*

Redcliffe - Redcliffe Quay *98-99*
    Robinson building *45*
    WCA Warehouse *96-97*
    City Council flats *39*
Redland - Ecohouse *106*
River Station *100-101*
Royal Fort - Physics Building *28*

St Augustine's Court/Parade *72*
St Bartholemew's Hospital *70-71*
St George - Air Balloon Schools *20*
St James's Parade - St James's Court *94*
St Monica Home of Rest *34-35*
St Stephen Street - old Times & Mirror *24*
Schools - Air Balloon *20*
    Badminton (library) *51*
    Lockleaze *43*
    Queen Elizabeth Hospital
    (theatre) *117*
Sea Mills - St Edyth's Church *35*
Shirehampton Village Hall *25*
Shot Tower *46*

Small Street - Crown Court *87*
Smeaton Road - B-Bond Warehouse *25*
    Ecohome *106*
Sneyd Park - Span housing *48*
Spike Island Centre *119*
Stoke Bishop - Wills Hall *36*
Stoke Gifford - Ministry of Defence *88-89*

Temple Quay *8*
Temple Way - Bristol United Press *60*
    Scottish Life building *61*

University buildings - Arts Faculty,
    Woodland Road *76*
    Chemistry Building (former) *23*
    Goldney residences *107*
    Merchant Venturer's Building/University
    Gate *95*
    Queen's Building *41*
    Physics Building *28*
    Senate House *50*
    Synthetic Chemistry *121*
    Wills Hall *36*
    Wills Memorial Building *27*

Vision Care Centre *6, 114*

Wapping Wharf *8*
Watershed *78-79*
Westbury-on-Trym -Concrete House *32*
    St Monica Home of Rest *34-35*
    Badminton School library *51*
Westbury Park - Carfax Court *77*
    Downs Park East *22*
Whitchurch - St Barnadette's Church *50*
White House *21*
Whiteladies Cinema *29*
Wildscreen @t Bristol *128*
Wills Hartcliffe *65*

Index of architects, designers, landscape architects and artists

Adams & Holden *16*
Alec French Partnership *8, 69, 70, 72, 73, 98, 104, 107, 114*
Appleton Group *116*
Architecton *97*
Artist Constructor *59*
Arup Associates *67, 83*
Arup, Ove & Partners *126*
Atkins Walters Webster Architects *95*

Balston & Co *76, 107, 124*
BBA *103*
BBC Architects *75*
Behnisch, Behnisch & Partner *8, 123*
BGP Group Architects/ Beardsworth Gallanaugh & Partners *66, 75, 116*
Bond, F Bligh *25*
Bristol City Architect's Department *39, 43*
Bristol City Council, City Centre Projects & Urban Design Team *86-87, 131*
Bristol City Council Leisure Services *115, 120*
Bristol City Council, Natural Environment Team *86*
Bruges Tozer Partnership *8, 106*
Bryan, Henry Dare *11, 21*
Building Design Partnership *93*

Casson Conder & Partners *51*

Cawthra, Hermon *37*
Chris Wilkinson Architects *129*
Clouston, Brian & Partners *90*
Concept Planning Group *124, 130*
Connell & Ward *6, 32*
Cowlin, Wiliam & Sons *25*
CPC *129*

DRG Architects *45*

Edwards Gale *84*
Ellis & Clarke *30*
Exedra D S Drage Architects *106*

Feilden Clegg Architects *8, 113*
Ferguson Mann Architects *53-55, 56, 77, 79, 118*
Foster & Wood *24*

Group Architects DRG *60, 61*

Harris, E Vincent *33*
Holden, Charles *14, 16*
Holden, Robert *90*
Holder Mathias Alcock *95*
Hopkins, Michael & Partners *128*
Hubbard Ford Partnership *84*

Inscape Architects *101*

Jakobsen Prebend *48*
JT Design Build *78*

Kenneth Nealon Tanner & Partners *50*
LaTrobe & Weston *18, 20, 29*
Lawrence & Wrightson *118*
Leonard Mannesseh/ LMP Architects *56, 108*
Love, Vic *84*

MacCormac Jamieson Prichard *76*
Malone, Kate *120*
Moxley Jenner & Partners *64, 70, 72-73*
Moxley Jenner Ltd *117*

Niall Phillips Architects *105, 119*
Nicholas Grimshaw & Partners *84*

Oatley, Sir George *6, 13, 23, 27, 28, 35, 36*
Oatley & Lawrence *23*
Oatley & Brentnall *41, 50*
O'Connell, Eilis *126*
John Outram Associates *90*

Percy Thomas Partnership *41, 62-63, 88-89, 115, 121*
Potter & Hare *49*
Priest, J L & Co *18*
PSA Landscape *87*

PTP Landscape *90*

Richard Pedlar Chartered Architects *70*
Randall-Page, Peter *120*
Ritchie, Walter *81*
Roques, A W *37*
Rodway & Dening *22*
Ross, Eric *42*

Scott, Sir Giles Gilbert *30, 37*
Skidmore Owings Merrill *65*
Stride Treglown Ltd *41, 72-73, 87*
Sudell & Waters *41*
Swann Associates, Peter *67, 83*

Thomas, Sir Percy & Son, see Percy
    Thomas Partnership
Thoday Associates, Peter *113*
Thorpe Architecture *90*
Thorpe, Philip *103*
Towning Hill & Partners *48*

Underwood, E N & Partners *46*
University of Bristol External Works
    Department *95, 121*
University of Bristol Gardens
    Department *95*

Ware, Peter *56, 70, 108, 110-111*
Watkins Gray & Partners *47*
Whicheloe Macfarlane Architects *47, 59*
Whinney, Son & Austen Hall *31*
Wilkinson see Chris Wilkinson Architects
Williams, Henry *17*

YRM *65*

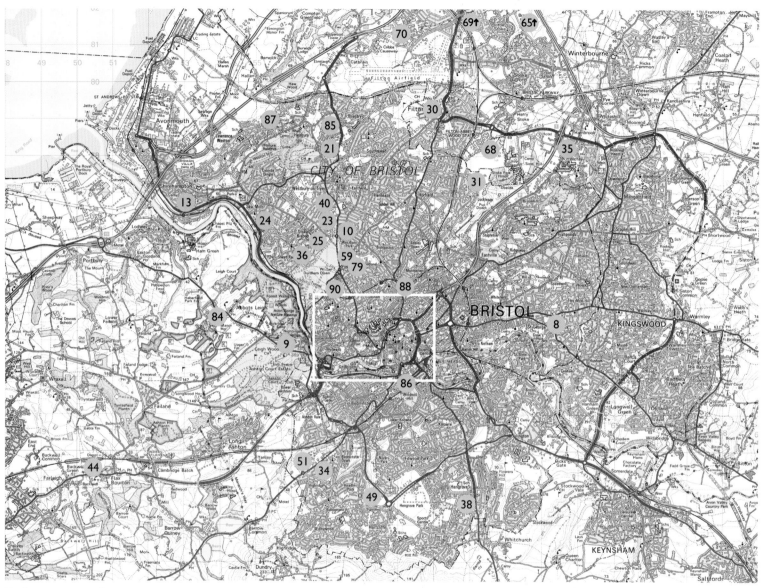

For key to map numbers, see page 140.

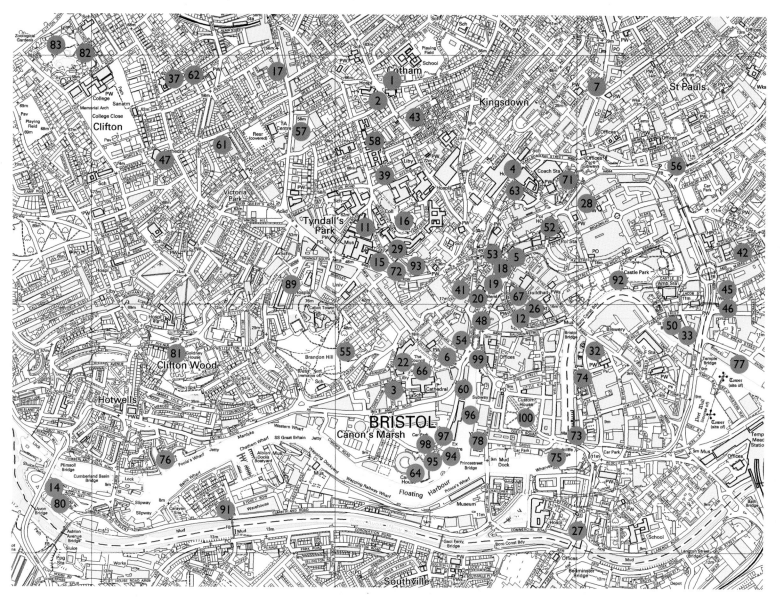

Key to maps

1. Former Western Congregational College, 1905-6, now The Family Practice (medical centre)
2. Former Homeopathic Hospital, 1908/1921
3. Central Library, 1906
4. Bristol Royal Infirmary (original building), 1906
5. Everard's Printing Works, 1900 now part of National Westminster Bank
6. former Cabot Cafe, 1900
7. Jamaica Street Carriage Works, 1905 and 1909
8. Air Balloon Schools, 1905
9. The White House, 1901
10. 42-44 Downs Park East, 1908
11. University of Bristol: Old Chemistry Building, 1909
12. Old Bristol Times & Mirror building 1904
13. Shirehampton Village Hall, 1904
14. B-Bond Warehouse, 1908
15. Wills Memorial Building, 1925
16. University Physics Building, 1929
17. Whiteladies Cinema, 1921
18. Royal Sun Alliance building (former Electricity Offices), 1938
19. Northcliffe House, circa 1929
20. Colston House, 1935
21. The Concrete House, 1934
22. The Council House, 1938
23. St Monica Home of Rest, 1928
24. St Edyth's Church, 1928
25. Wills Hall, 1925
26. Fresco Italian Brasserie, 1935
27. City Council Flats, Redcliffe, 1950+
28. Former Lewis's Department Store, 1957 now Bentall's
29. Queen's Building, 1958
30. Brabazon Assembly Hall, 1949
31. Lockleaze Secondary School, 1954+
32. One Redcliff Street, 1964

33. Shot Tower, 1968
34. Bristol Water head office, 1963
35. Manor Park Estate, 1959 onwards
36. Span housing, 1965
37. All Saints Church, 1967
38. St Bernadette RC Church, 1968
39. University of Bristol Senate House, 1962
40. Library, Badminton School, 1969
41. Inner city repair and renewal c1978-1985
42. Old Market: conservation and renewal, 1977 onwards
43. High Kingsdown, 1974
44. Five Houses, Flax Bourton, 1973
45. Bristol United Press, 1972
46. Scottish Life Building, 1976
47. Clifton Cathedral, 1974
48. Colston Centre, 1973
49. Wills Hartcliffe, 1977
50. Wessex House, 1976
51. The Pavilions (formerly CEGB SW Region headquarters), 1978
52. One Bridewell Street, 1987
53. Renewal and Conservation: a. Centre Gate House; b. St Bartholemew's Hospital; c. St Bartholemew's; d. Christmas Steps and Colston Street, 1982-1990
54. St Augustine's Parade, St Augustine's Court, c.1988-1990
55. No 31 Great George Street, 1987
56. Spectrum, 1984
57. BBC Regional Headquarters, 1987
58. University of Bristol Arts Faculty, 1985
59. Carfax Court, 1989
60. Watershed (re-use of transit sheds), 1982
61. Stonewest House, 1983
62. Garden Court, 1983
63. Brick Sculpture, Bristol Eye Hospital, 1986
64. Lloyds Bank Headquarters, 1992
65. RAC Bradley Stoke Supercentre, 1994
66. College Green refurbishment, 1991

67. Bristol Crown Court, 1994
68. Ministry of Defence Procurement Executive, 1996
69. Aztec West, 1981 onwards
70. The Mall, 1998
71. St James's Court, 1996
72. Merchant Venturers Building/University Gate, 1996
73. WCA Warehouse conversion, 1997
74. Redcliffe Quay, 1991
75. River Station, 1998
76. Poole's Wharf, 1999
77. Marketing & Exhibition Centre, 1992
78. The Architecture Centre, 1996
79. Ecohouse, 1997
80. Ecohome, Cumberland Basin, 1996
81. Goldney Hall student residences, 1996
82. Bristol Zoo: Canopy and Restaurant, 1992
83. Bristol Zoo: Entrance Building, 1996
84. The Beeches, 1996
85. Bengough House, 1997
86. Vision Care Centre, 1993
87. Orlebar Gardens affordable housing, 1995 and 1997
88. Housing for Vietnamese refugees, 1995
89. QEH Theatre, 1990
90. Old Vic Theatre School: new Dance Studio, 1995
91. Spike Island Centre, 1998
92. Public art in Castle Park, 1993
93. University of Bristol Synthetic Chemistry Building, 1999
94. Harbourside Centre, abortive
95. Millennium Square, 2000
96. Pero's Bridge, 1999
97. Wildscreen @t Bristol, 2000
98. Explore @t Bristol, 200
99. Reviving The Centre, 2000
100. Queen Square restored, 2000-2002